Other Books by Terry Atkinson

Paths of Righteousness in Psalm 23
The Growing Pains of Peter
Peter: The Mature Man
In Sickness and in Health
Dying Is Living
Buried Talents
Diamonds in David
More than Conquerors
Dwarfing Giants
The Word of Knowledge in Action
Living with a Prophetess
The Blood of God's Son, Jesus Christ
A Miner's Minor, Volume 1
A Miner's Minor, Volume 2
Prevailing Prayer

BRUISED

but Not

BROKEN

The Story of the Bruised Reed

TERRY ATKINSON

WESTBOW
PRESS®
A DIVISION OF THOMAS NELSON
& ZONDERVAN

WestBow Press books may be ordered through booksellers or by contacting:

WestBow Press
A Division of Thomas Nelson & Zondervan
1663 Liberty Drive
Bloomington, IN 47403
www.westbowpress.com
844-714-3454

Unless otherwise noted, all scripture quotations are taken from the King James Version of the Bible.

Scripture marked J.B. Phillips taken from the J.B. Phillips Modern New Testament.

Scripture quotations marked MSG are taken from THE MESSAGE, copyright © 1993, 2002, 2018 by Eugene H. Peterson. Used by permission of NavPress. All rights reserved. Represented by Tyndale House Publishers, a Division of Tyndale House Ministries.

ISBN: 978-1-6642-2171-0 (sc)
ISBN: 978-1-6642-2173-4 (hc)
ISBN: 978-1-6642-2172-7 (e)

Library of Congress Control Number: 2021901866

Print information available on the last page.

WestBow Press rev. date: 02/24/2021

This book is dedicated to those who have suffered. I am praying that through reading it, they might find the ointment of grace.

A broken reed he will not bruise.

—Matthew 12:20

We are troubled on every side, yet not distressed;
we are perplexed but not in despair.

—2 Corinthians 4:8

Knocked down but not knocked out.

—*J. B. Philipps Translation of the New Testament*

But Stephen, full of the Holy Spirit, hardly
noticed—he had eyes only for God.

—Acts 7:55 (MSG)

I'll make all my mountains into roads,
turn them into superhighways.

—Isaiah 49:11 (MSG)

Contents

Introduction

Bruised but Not Broken is a different type of book compared to another book I wrote about human suffering. It is the story of the bruised-but-not-broken reed, taken from Matthew 12:20. It's a story and also an allegory of the Christian life, and it answers many of the questions about why we suffer. Written during the COVID-19 pandemic of 2020, this book seeks to explain why we sometimes suffer, and it will bring light and understanding to the heart and to our sometimes-muddled intellect. When darkness falls, this book will help you look for the shining moon, and when day breaks, it will help you look for the rising sun and to rise with it.

What is it that keeps a ship afloat when it is passing through a storm? What unique things keep it from going onto the rocks or into the deep abyss? It's not because of its metal fabrication or shape. Such strong waves can tear the rivets apart. Modern communications and the ability to send out an SOS can assist. It's not the strengthened steel, the riveted bulwarks, its shape, or its ability that brings it through a hurricane. The decks and rails can be like butter.

The crew might be healthy and strong, but they are only part of the success. The sailor's portion of rum is wasted at this time. The ship has its Plimsoll line, but this is no help as the storm rages. These things can help. What bring it through any storm are the Captain, our Lord, and His good crew, who know through experience what to do to avoid calamity and sinking. The Captain has to take the ship, with crew intact from sinking or swimming, into survival mode.

His experience begins to tell as they pass through what would have passed through them.

There will be moments, for many of sheer pain married to frustration, that are determined to pronounce the death sentence over you. You will feel as if pins of pain have stuck into parts of your body. What brings us through any prolonged period of personal suffering is a calm reliance on God, who said to the raging sea, "Peace, be still," meaning, "Be muzzled!" (Mark 4:39), as if He were controlling a mad dog. Only God can make a rope out of the water and pull you to safety and into peace, using that cord as a cord of love that lifts you above the storm. You can be brought into "Abraham's Bosom" (Luke 16:22), describing where ships went in a time of the storm until the storm had passed. You can go through bruising and suffering from wreck to rectify and then to the right.

Life will throw many things at us, and sometimes it includes the kitchen sink. At times like this, we don't need to falter or fail. Within the bruising God allows, any doctor will tell you there is the element of healing. This is a type of self-help that comes from the wounded hands of the Savior, Jesus Christ.

You may feel like you are a born loser, but the Master intends that you go on to be a winner in all classes and cases. As you read this book, *Bruised but Not Broken,* you will find a pattern and path you can follow that will bring you to the winning line with everything intact. You will be made stronger by the power of His might.

Here are promises from God to you:

"But I'll take the hand of those who don't know the way, who can't see where they are going. I'll be a personal guide to them, directing them through unknown country" (Isaiah 42:16 MSG). Let Isaiah's words become your guide through every painful pinch. "But Thou has loved my soul delivered it from a pit of corruption" (Isaiah 38:17).

One
The Need for the Musical Reed

M arriage can be a wonderful thing, especially when it is made in heaven and reflects heaven on earth. To maintain a good marriage, you soon realize how well balanced a man and woman are. They have different qualities to contribute to perfect bliss. The man can minister to the woman, and the woman can minister to the man; their differences are found in the shepherd and the reed. There would be an ongoing relationship with a reed found. Their association if the leader of lambs found the perfect tube would be of everlasting value.

When one was weak, the other held them up. When the other felt frail, it was the music from the reed that brought heavy feet back into the line of duty. The need for the man of animals was something that could touch him so he could touch others. This man of quality required the quality of a reed to lift his drooping spirits. When he felt too tired to reach and pull himself up by his shoelaces, he required a helping third hand—the river reed.

Through the teachings and experiences of life, you realize you require more than self-help. You need something alongside you that becomes your other half. If you feel that "destiny's child" describes you, then you will require the equivalent of what you are to complement you. The hammer is the extension of your arm, what you think is sister and brother of the deed. Wearing spectacles adds

1

to your eyes. All of us desire something that will complement who we are.

In every realm, we desire and need a friend who sticks closer than a brother (Proverbs 18:24). We need that extra hand, a surplus to help us when we are running on low. Throughout life, we wear clothing, shoes, hairstyles, and makeup to complement what we are. We desire to become more than the bare necessities of life. Elohim clothed Adam and Eve (Genesis 3:21).

When the train moves into or out of the station, the stationmaster uses his tin whistle as a complement to what he is and has. That tin whistle is like the green reed the isolated herdsman would use. The red or green flag is there to assist the whistle of the stationmaster. Where one might fail, the other works as it complements it. Another instrument used before trains were lost, going over the hills and far away, was the sledgehammer. It was used in a ceremony against the engine and coach wheels to see if they were reliable. These additions were used to complement both the person and the train.

These articles were the weapons of the stationmaster to keep the trains progressing and people moving. These tools got them to move to a schedule, a pattern that had already been arranged. Our weapons aren't carnal in our warfare. We use these weapons as the reed is used—not bells, whistles, green or red flags, or even a swinging hammer. They are "mighty through God, to the pulling down of strongholds" (2 Corinthians 10:4).

It was God who added flowers to stems. He placed strong and thick boughs on trees so each branch could bear fruit as an addition and multiplication to what the tree is. The branch isn't the tree, and the tree isn't the branch. God has set everything in its proper order (1 Corinthians 15:23). In the human body, everything has been set in order. That is so everything can work together for our good (Romans 8:28).

It was this working together that the shepherd and reed pipe experienced, doing what the other couldn't do. One was lost without the other. The pipe reed took the sheep shearer out of himself, creating another world—the world of music. One note of melody sounding into the dry dust made it appear as if water ran through. What was wrecked by time and tread was converted into another use.

Throughout the Bible, you will be amazed by what small things God used as complements. His grace worked through them. These things were His cruet set of vinegar, salt, pepper, and mustard. From one word, He created light (Genesis 1:3). "Let there be light" is all one word: light. Using the dust of the earth, He created Adam (Genesis 1:26–27). Using a woman's rib, man was created.

Through one person, sin came into the world (Romans 5:12). Through that same man, the nations of the world were born. Through one man, Abraham, the nations of the world were blessed (Romans 4:17). Through one word, *repent*, people come to Christ (Acts 17:30). He used the jawbone of an ass (Judges 15:16–18). The oxen goad became an instrument of deliverance from oppression (Judges 3:31). Small arrows were used—not for flight or fight but to fulfill a prophecy (2 Kings 13:15–17).

It was through one reed found by a river or stream that the longings of the sheep feeder were assuaged. When God created man and woman in Genesis, He provided them with hands, feet, mouths, ears to hear, and legs to walk. If used as the reed by the man who led creatures, they will add to you and not take away. Using your legs, you will walk. Using your hands, you will give and take. With your heart, you will love. Eyes enable you to see and avoid stumbling. Hands receive and give. All these were requirements that took humankind further and deeper into Eden's garden. It was only by using these accompaniments that people began to multiply and subdue the earth (Genesis 1:28).

Some things are complementary, while others are necessities. We require both; just as the shepherd required his sheep, he also needed the cut reed. Only if it were cut did it produce music. When the shepherd injured his leg in a fall, it was the reed that came to help him stand firm. We tend to depend on weak things when we are weak. We appreciate the light only when in the depths of darkness.

Running water is appreciated during thirst. As the star requires the night sky, so this shepherd required the reed. It would become the book of his writing. It became his alter ego.

The lot of the Eastern man wasn't easy. There were moments of contemplation as he gazed into the glowing embers. In his mind, he could see figures emerging from the flames. He saw armies conquering many nations. He thought he saw bears and lions coming to take his sheep away into the land of forgetfulness. He saw what he lived day by day. In the sizzling of the branches, he thought he could hear music; the music of consolation for his chafed spirit was like the balm of Gilead being rubbed deeply into his hurts (Jeremiah 8:22; 51:8).

You Can Be in a Crowd and Be Lonely

He realized he could be in a group and yet be lonely. Loneliness added to his isolation. He was at the center of the sheep, but he was there only for what the sheep could obtain from him—at the center but in his heart—beyond the circumference of comfort. The sheep brought no consolation because they couldn't hold a human conversation with him. He was like a desert island: left, vacated, and forgotten.

On other occasions, there were moments of despair when he lost a sheep. There were seconds of sheer terror as he leaned over the cliff's edge with his crook to rescue the wanderer. When the sheep moved from pasture to pasture, there was much hurrying, scurrying, and rushing. Despondency and depression always awaited him around the next hillock, ready to ambush him and take him captive, dragging him away while screaming and crying.

THERE ARE ALWAYS BETTER DAYS AHEAD

In his better days and more joyful moods, the shepherd knew where he was going, but the sheep didn't. Usually, red-letter days were followed by black days of despair and dungeon incarceration. This illustrates the fact that you should leave your future in God's hands, and if you do, you will become more than a wanderer or complainer. Be a sailing ship or even a seesaw rather than a rotting piece of wood. When we don't know where to go, we need to go to our pathways' leader, the all-knowing, all-caring Jesus Christ, who beckons. He planned the universe (Colossians 1:16), so you can depend on Him to plan your life.

He has this universe measured between his thumb and little finger. If left to yourself, life becomes a plot or scheme. There has been many a scream in a human scheme. There are times when life seems to be a long plod, but left to Christ, it can be a pattern that is part of a plan. In Psalm 23:3, we have the words "paths of righteousness." The true meaning of those words is "right paths." Every shepherd was known for the right courses he chose for his sheep. There never was a shepherd like our Shepherd, who not only chooses the right paths for us but is also the way, truth, and life (John 14:6). Other ways may be made out of the grass, soil, clay, or stone; but our way is a living way that speaks to us as we journey.

YOUR MUSICAL ABILITY HEARD THROUGH YOUR WORSHIP

The musical reed, if the shepherd possessed one, was with the shepherd and kept in his clothes near to his heart. The shepherd badly needed one now. It was sometimes better than a sharp weapon. Without the musical reed, he was always open to attack—not from a lion or bear but from things that would attack his spirit. It could kill anguish, fear, and uncertainty through its music. He illustrates what God thinks of our praise and worship. Get on your knees, for your musical ability is heard in your worship and praise. On your knees, you feel like you are going nowhere, but as you worship (as with a reed pipe), you are going everywhere, because scenes of home and delightful places pass through the shepherd's mind as he plays the pastoral pipe.

Moments of regret are turned into opportunities. Clouds of doubt are dispelled by the spell of music; rainclouds are converted into rainbows. In some circumstances, to beat off attacking animals and other things that would destroy the sheep, the shepherd had to lay down his life for the sheep (John 10:11). That life became a bridge into eternity.

TRY SINGING AND WORSHIPPING FOR OVERCOMING

The marauders were beat off by the dulcet tones of the music coming from the reed. This shepherd could play more tunes on his reed than he could count sheep. This reed music was sometimes better than an open fire.

Try singing and worshipping for overcoming. It was the life of the shepherd, who led the wandering sheep from this side of turbulent waters to the other side, where the streams were musical. It was to these flowing streams that his reed of readiness was taken and tuned. Fear or turbulent waters weren't music but sent to retune his heart. In the midst or at the side of the most turbulent stream, his music could sound out as a leading instrument player in any recital. He badly needed a reed as the ointment of graces.

ISOLATION AND LONELINESS ARE SO TRICKY

Being a shepherd was a lonely affair, divorced from human companionship. It can be a love affair but with only you as the lover. Self-love always leads to self-pity and a pool of water you drown in. Without a pastoral reed, his loneliness was as deep as any sea and as wide as an ocean, the isolation not drowned in the seven seas or the oceans of the world.

Loneliness and isolation can be so different, and there is no relationship in loneliness. Loneliness is different from isolation. You can be lonely in a crowd, just as the sheep keeper was lonely with his sheep. He required something that couldn't be obtained from sheep leading, carrying, or caring. Every day seemed as if yesterday was tomorrow, and it had canceled itself, and today with its clouded emotions reigned supreme forever, in the grip of a gripe as he wistfully thought and complained to the sheep. What could they do? The only musical thing they knew was a constant repetition of their call?

Every Day Was like a Furrowed Field

Every day was like a furrow in a field—straight, shallow, and long; shallow but not deep. The furrow was like a grave; the only difference was the depth. Furrows are where things grow, but there is no growth in that feeling of being alone with only the stars to play with and rivers as companions. How many rocks had he counted today? How many blades of grass had he sought to gauge, as if each blade were a sheep?

As he thought, just as you feel, he became only more lonely in isolation. The shepherd without a reed of music felt the world was closing in on him. As it did so, it squeezed his spirit dry until there was no paint left in his mind for paintings that would delight him. Even his memory sometimes seemed like a closed book, sealed with many seals (Revelation 5:1) and locked by depression. That is why, as we gaze into the ashes of our asking, we seek, begging for something to stir us up, and it makes us take hold of what the Lord wants to take hold of us for. Like this sheep leader, we invent mock battles and pretend we are fighting a war that never existed.

Loneliness is terrible; it is the brother and sister of helplessness and the cousin of emptiness. Sometimes the only companions the shepherd in Israel had were the particles of grit in the dust, but these were far away. He felt as trodden on as each piece of a small rock in the uneven and unsure pathway. The moon was canceled; somebody had forgotten to light the stars. The river was there as his entertainment, but it always seemed to flow in the same direction, the wrong way; it was still flowing away from him. There were certain things the shepherd could do in his isolation.

HE COULD INVENT GAMES

Gazing into a stream or pond, he could pray. The provider could play a guessing game, of which sheep would bear a lamb first. He would design games with sticks to see which piece of wood would burn for the longest time. How many times had he counted his sheep? To while away the night hours, he played with small stones from his pouch, trying to throw them into a small hole. Countless times he had counted the number of fingers on his hands. It was no entertainment to count the sheep or blades of grass. In that boredom, he would listen and see whether he could discern the difference between each sheep's voices.

He soon realized that, as God had ordained, every bleat of every sheep was different, just as every cluck of a hen had meaning to it. In his isolation, he counted the snowflakes as they fell onto the ground. Deep in his heart, the leader of the sheep felt that he must find something that would cut like a sharp knife through his feeling of loneliness. He thought the thief had come to steal, rob, and destroy (John 10:10) not the sheep but his soul. Something was required that would sentence this feeling of despair to death.

Maybe, just maybe, if he found a reed by the riverside and converted the water that had swirled by it into music, that might meet his requirements. He knew from experience that when logs of wood sometimes burn, poetically the noises that come from them as they are devoured by fire can be the voices of young lovers, who have sat under the branches of the tree. The song reed he would choose contained the melodies of the stream. As water flowed by, the sounds of the waters were all imprisoned within the reed pipe. If he could find one and take it captive through specific methods, he could release the music in it. It would take the cutting of the knife and the piercing of the reed to accomplish this. It could be the finest moment of both sheep rescuer and grass reed.

Two

The Search for the Musical Reed

You may be wondering why I am telling you about the requirements of the shepherd and his deep longing and association with music as developed in a reed? Everything I have written in the history of the reed is your history. Some have diaries that contain dark days. A day in the life of the shepherd of the sheep can be like a day in your life. There are days and hours when it seems as if the sun and stars don't appear for many days. Many a time, many a day, has been in "the deep" (2 Corinthians 11:25), the deep of frustration, where everything seems to not only seem wrong but also to go wrong and could go wrong. Nothing can be right because it is wrong. Nothing seems right, and even a cup of tea doesn't taste right. Every night seems to be a fortnight. It is an ill wind that blows nobody any good.

The short life of the reed is your life. Like you, it was found to be brought in as an assistant to worship. The shepherd seeks earnestly day and night—by the second, hour, or minute—for a reed. So Jesus Christ has pursued you, to put into your heart not only music but also majesty and glory. In the hands of the leader, the reed expanded from the riverside into something that could be useful. The prize, the ability of the shepherd, went into the reed. The days of boredom and isolation were to cease. New hope is in life when God takes hold of you (2 Corinthians 3:12). As the shepherd searches, there's suddenly that moment of revelation when he sees the reed in its muddy circumstances. It's just an ordinary river flag; it can act as a trumpet, flute, mouth organ, or club. To lean on it, you would do so at your peril because it is so weak. It doesn't seem to have or be of any use. Its only usefulness appears to be in decoration, and that doesn't amount to much. There it is, swaying in the wind like a drunken man, going to and fro. You can't expect too much from the mud. There is nothing to commend it or to make it distinctive. There is no bright yellow or red flower growing from it.

THE SHEPHERD FELT HIS LIFE LACKED SOME OOMPH

The next step for the sheep carer wasn't to lead sheep but to go to deep waters and find a reed that would help to bring something and someone back to life. Finding it would be like finding a long, lost friend. Would this be like a magic wand, and could he be like the Fairy Godmother? That reed, if found, could give his heart the "kiss of life." New light came into his eyes as he "eyed" it. His feet would find their youthful spring again. Maybe the skip and frolic of the lamb would be injected into him.

Feeling that his life requires a "kick start," he began to search high and low. Not any old reed would meet the need. It is strange that for his future victories, he chose a thing defined as weak (2 Kings 18:21). It wasn't to the strong, swift, or capable that he went but to what was so vulnerable that he couldn't build with it or use it as a staff. The thought came into his empty mind; maybe he was, in choosing, a weak thing of this world (1 Corinthians 1:27).

Terry Atkinson

GOD ALWAYS LOOKS FOR THAT WITHOUT SHAPE OR FUTURE

The reed the shepherd searched for lacked in design or shape; he would make it his very own, using his hands (Adam's carpentry) to shape it into what he wanted it to be. It didn't matter where it was or where he had found it. He would put his heart, body, soul, and spirit into it. That found became his machine. In another world and at another time, it was a spring lamb. There would be more design in it than any great temple building. It would be to the sheep keeper as the only one in the universe, just as you are to God. He would make it what God has made you, one of his "very own peculiar people" (1 Peter 2:9). The leader would have to wind the reed to bring the best music from it. When we illustrate that process through pain and hurt, we see that the best is brought from us. When the palette knife scrapes into the paint, beautiful pictures appear.

If it was human, how many times would the reed have thought, *Why does this have to be so? Why the piercing of my life and the pain? Is there any pattern in the problem?* Can the surgeon's knife or scalpel be the artist's knife when applying the oil paint to a masterpiece? Who but God can put a silver lining into depression? It is the Lord who can kiss a dull rain cloud with gold.

This water reed would be of great design and become its designer's reed of music, the master of ceremonies. Another nature rather than Mother Nature would turn it into an instrument of fine-tuning. Another hand, different from the hand of nature, would take hold of it and cause it to grow into other dimensions. It would become a child of his grace. Yet to pour grace into it, this stick would have to be wounded and converted. It would have to be pierced through with many sorrows, just as Jesus Christ was (Isaiah 53:5–6).

The Sheep Leader Needed Something More

He needed to find something that would mean more to him than his sheep, crook, or staff. He seemed to have everything he required to shepherd sheep. Sometimes those who seem to have everything in truth have nothing. What they have can hide what they haven't got. Empty shells are discovered only on inspection, telling you there is no pearl here. The bleat of the sheep was replaced by the sweet music of the valleys and hills. He cared for the sheep, one by one and in a flock, but he required something he could make into music.

There was a desire in the heart of the sheep keeper to translate the sounds of nature. How could a branch, being broken, become a musical note?

He could never dance with sheep. He wanted something found in the reed that would set his heart on fire, and his feet dancing in the dust of the valley. It would discover the joy in both reed and leader of sheep, something that would make the trees and hills now skip with the lambs, illustrating the fact that you, committing yourself into the hands of Christ to be carved, cared for, and reshaped, even redefined, aren't a chance thing.

Jesus came, seeking and looking for you (Matthew 18:11). Jesus came where you were to make you what He is. The pipe became part of the craftsmanship of this leader, so you are part of the word and work of the carpenter of Nazareth. His loving care and seeking heart take care and act as an ointment of grace. The reed was pierced, hurt, crushed, and designed for a new life in an original purpose. Never think of yourself as just a thing of chance but only the one He was seeking. What the precious jewel is to the lapidary or the gem is to the jeweller, you are to the Christ of God.

Terry Atkinson

A Reed Was a Picture of Instability

A reed was always an emblem of weakness, as weak as the water it grew in. John the Baptist, some thought, was like a reed blowing this way and that in the wind (Matthew 11:7) and was ultimately swept away into thoughtlessness. It isn't the pipe that had power. The power required was in the hands of the lamb lover. That is why Egypt, in its weakness, is described as a reed (2 Kings 18:21), as weak as a reed, so that when someone leans on it for support, it crumbles into nothing.

You can't lean on the reed, but you can learn music on it. There aren't too many uses for a reed. Jesus in His glory and splendor has come to you, because, as much as the shepherd requires music, Jesus needs you, acquires you, and bring you to himself. The glory you lack He places in you. After finding you, He has work to do in you, so Jesus might work through you.

We Need to Be Devoted to the Cause of Christ

There was a need in the heart of the shepherd for more than what he already had. Small animals he led count be counted and pastured, but he required a thing that couldn't be counted. He didn't want to possess things (Isaiah 36:8). He wanted something that would keep him, a reed to which he could devote himself. This would be his lamb, offered on the altar of nature, a chosen reed to become his one-man band with the shepherd as the musician. He required some pastoral music found in a rustic reed. If music is the "food of love" he was hungry, starving, but even a freshly carved roasted sheep wouldn't meet the feeling of deep-down hunger. This hunger painted no pictures of a picnic or a little bird eating crumbs. It was of banquet proportions—you know, the same feast provided for the returning prodigal son (Luke 15:23). He longed for the sweet taste of the music of the spheres, hence the shepherd's pipe.

There are parts of the makeup of a human only music can reach. Music digs where no spade can come, shining where no sunbeam can shine. It reaches beyond starry sky at night. He required tunes as fingers to go into the center of his being and scrape out all the doubt and despair. He needed music at midnight as Paul and Silas did in Acts 16:25.

The enemy that reigned there must be disposed and revealed as the despot that he was. He wanted to dance the dance of the Hebrew boy in his heart. He wanted something more than that coming from the sounds of the stream or the call of a bird. The roar of a lion or bear brought no consolation, only fear off the lead as a charging bull or a swooping eagle. He wanted the music to soothe his soul and sing out his praises to anything and everything that had "ears to hear." They were the things around him that became his tuning fork. The pitch of the tube of music would be by the familiar sounds of falling rocks, screeching birds, and meandering streams.

THE CRACKLING OF BURNING WOOD ISN'T MUSICAL

The loneliness for the hillside shepherd was almost unbearable. It feels as if an unseen hand was slowly strangling him. If ever he had been placed on a torture wrack, this was his. Where could he find music with all its charms? This flute would become the instrument of his salvation. When and where the moon didn't and couldn't shine, the flute commanded everything. Another creation was born in his spirit. The reed, through its music, said, "Light!" And light appeared (Genesis 1:3). It was like a Roman centurion. It said to do this (Luke 7:8), and it happened. The sheep-shepherd was as one with the authority of music in him, the leader working through it, just as the power of Christ would work through you (Ephesians 1:19). A word of command accomplished it through this slender tunnel. Light streamed from every note played as the pasture man entered the valley of death. Here would be the key to every prison cell and the opening of every locked door that stood in his way. "Away darkness and fear!" it said. This music was the final whistle in the game of life. Lengthening evening shadows play no music, only tricks on the mind. What was distorted and wrecked, it brought back into shape. Here was the hand of the potter, shaping the clay into something beautiful and useful.

There isn't any music in the breaking of a stick. If rubbed together, the posts can bring heat and warmth to the body, but there was a deep requirement in the pastor's spirit—assurance in warmth when tones tumbled from the reed as playful children. The crackling of burning wood isn't musical. The wandering nomad listens to the whistle of the stone as it flies from the sling. Every bird call is so hollow when compared with what couldn't be in the most bottomless well or river. If he had some musical instrument, he could at least charm snakes. If he possessed a trumpet, he could sound a note that would echo across the valley, calling, commanding men to go, rallying behind their leader for better or worse. Israel, as a nation, had their silver trumpet and ram's horn, but he didn't possess even a tin whistle (Joshua 6:5; Numbers 10:2).

The Things That Surround Can Surmount Us

Thoughts tumble through his head as sand running through the fingers. The only problem and difference are this sand did not keep flowing through his fingers. It usually, as tormenting thoughts in his mind, remain stuck between finger and thumb.

Jesus would warn against building on sand (Matthew 7:26), sand as unstable and unreliable as any reed. The only music he had at that moment was his ability to whistle to the flames of fire at nighttime. The arrow in flight, as the sharpening of the knife, has no musical repertoire in it. Then, as day breaks, the leader of the sheep begins to hum a tune. If only this lonely one could play it on an instrument; hence the need for a reed. Tongue, breath, and teeth through his mouth are imperfect substitutes. The birds can make musical sounds, but these are of little consolation to the soul hungry for music. The dawn chorus signals the midnight hour as depression sets in as concrete in the mind. In this state of mind, even the dawn chorus is out of tune. He begins in his isolation to throw pebbles into the stream. They offer no sacrifice of music on the altar of his lonely, wandering spirit. He listens for the music any stream will produce as it meanders around rocks and stones. There is no music in the snapping of the twig or the baying of the wolf. He has all these things, but there is a more profound longing in his spirit for a whole symphony for his sympathy. He begins to think aloud as they come near a stream; there is something here that could be the rhythm of the music.

THINGS SEEN ARE SYMBOLS OF MET NEEDS

There are types and shadows in the experiences of the reed pipe. These are found in our experiences with God. The artificer sees things "through a glass darkly" (seeing everything through mud and dirty water) to being made known as it was known (1 Corinthians 13:12). All the darkness of a long night of fear and suffering is taken away in one moment. There will be no more anguish or languishing in a pool of dirty water. Life will no longer be like drinking dirty water from a pool. That which is useless is made useful as an unearthed musical talent. Let these "shadows" be "substance" (Hebrews 11:1). "Substance" is the title "deed." Let this water be a wine that has been produced by the Master's touch (John 2:2–11). That touch is the touch of the zephyr. It is the hand that is different from the howling storm and crashing wind. This hand is graceful. It doesn't open to release thunder and forked lightning. It is the hand that contains a necklace made up of superlatives.

The fingers are the reed's hand of destiny. This working, sculpting hand is the hand of dexterity and destiny. It is the hand of the shepherd but with so many talents hidden in it. Sweet music would sound from its hollow existence. The music pipe experiences the cutting edge of the knife that would shape it. What nature does when cutting and carving flowers into reality, this hand would consist of for the pipe. The vagrancies of the weather have shaped it so far in life. More than wind, rain or snow, stream or river, another power as found in the hand of the shepherd would carve it.

Three

Finding the Musical Reed

What was it that made the shepherd seek, stop, and stoop to save the bruised reed? It was a matter of sovereign choice. The man of the valleys had no choice when a lamb was born. He received what was given to him, but this choice of a musical instrument was different. To save it, the shepherd had to come down to the level of the pastoral reed. He had to come just where it was to rescue it as it was. His stretching of the arm as his grasping by the hand must be adequate. It was a heart of love that contained more power and purpose than the stream had. No pelting rain or strong winds, not even soft winds, would produce in it what the leader of the sheep would create. His hand was the production line, and it had only this one product, required for such a time and season as this. What the shepherd was about to do would turn the clock back from the midnight hour to the former dawn. The night would become day with a laugh on its face.

It was found, designed, and loved above other reeds. It was a choice in the matter of choosing (Ephesians1:5, 11). When he saw it, it was an abandoned wreck, a boat without water. Without the mastery of the master, it would just be any old reed. Broken, it could only float on the surface of the water to an uncertain and unknown destination. It would have represented a reed coracle, grounded, up the creek without a paddle! What was it about this "ground organ" that he loved? In another life and other circumstances, it might have been a "grand organ." Even though it had grown lower down, it contained no music in the lower or minor key, no piece of any kind without the help of the shepherd. He could make it sing. There were qualities in this stick nature had placed there that could be taken and released through music.

Christ brings every life surrendered to Him back into tune (2 Corinthians 5:18–19). He stirs the slumbering chords again.

CHRIST GOES TO THE BOTTOM OF THE PILE

The love that leans the lowest finds the lowest and crowns it with new aspirations. Let me remind you that when Jesus Christ found us, there was no merit in us, who were made of mud and blood. We were sinking, some quicker than others. We weren't the tallest or best reeds on the riverbank. We weren't the tallest but the smallest. Easily crushed by a human hand, it was a human hand that caused it to grow beyond riverbank or swirling waters.

The musical reed, coming from the heart of the shepherd, was sought by the same shepherd. When he found it, he felt an upward tug, more potent than the downward spiral. It had the marks of being "downtrodden" when nature through wind, sun, and storm sought to influence it. Hence, where he found it, it was at the bottom and not at the top. When things surround you, you feel you are sinking, and there is no deeper depth for you to descend to, look for and find a loving hand that has come to your rescue.

Peter, beginning to sink, cried, "Lord, save me!" (Matthew 14:30). It is the hand of help, the hand of the handyman, the hand of a faithful musician who wants to stir slumbering cords and move across your heart again until your life becomes a symphony of worship, a symphony of sympathy for others, who have fallen as you have. What made God choose you (2 Thessalonians 2:13)? What made you the "choice" in His choosing? You were never, and would never have been, determined by the wisdom of this world with its sandcastles.

THE SHEPHERD FOUND THE PERFECT REED

It was with great endeavor and difficulty that the shepherd found the perfect reed, which required him to play music. It wasn't perfect in that it had no faults, and it grew straight up, toward heaven and the blue sky. There was no style in the pipe style but the love of the hand that reached for it. There were enough love and strength in that hand to transform a thousand reeds. That same hand of God had parted rivers and seas (Numbers 21:14).

After a long search, he finally finds the very thing he feels will meet the need, his need, and it will complete the longing of his heart. This particular reed seemed to be the missing piece in his puzzle of life. Why he chose one reed above another, nobody will ever know. The reed, being hollow and empty, would allow sweet music to fill the air. His choice came because it was empty. It had no merit of its own. All it would ever be would be what the man of quiet waters would make of it—it chose to be collected and cut because it had little resistance to what the finder required to do with it. The secret of being taken and used by God isn't to resist.

LOVE FILLS THE GAP BETWEEN YOU AND YOUR CREATOR

There was a great gulf between the leader of the sheep and the reed. He had to stretch to reach it. He had to come to it. These things explain why Christ, the shepherd on a cross, died with outstretched hands. He was saying to all, like this reed, as this shepherd who had been worn and weary, heavy laden, "Come unto me, and I will give you rest" (Matthew 11:28). His desire, his love could only fill that gap.

It took two hands, two feet, the obedience of a divine order to rescue you. With the ground flooded, the reed was in deep waters. As the storm raged in deep trouble, it was more profound than the waters that flowed by. Can you imagine the struggle the shepherd had to get to the reed and make it into a Moses, meaning "drawn from many waters"? Each step he took might be his last. The muddy riverbed could soon give way under his weight. What was planned as a rescue mission could have become a mission into misery and hurt.

The shepherd's feet would be hurt as he trod across the stream to get to the other side, where the reed was. The riverbed was uneven. The pathway he walked was on one of the rough surfaces, since rocks and large stones had been deposited here through the years. The reed sometimes grew among thorns, and as the shepherd reached out to take it, those thorns would pierce his hands. Blood and water dripped from him. The reed would be blood stained and blood claimed. It marked him as he sought to rescue the reed. This musical tune would be saved at a high cost and hurt to the sheep keeper.

The Shadow of a Cross Depicted on the Water

As he reached among a thorny bush growing on the banks of the river, thorns would almost hide the head of the rescuer and Creator. As he stretched out his arms across the water, the shadow of a cross appeared on the surface.

If you looked at the scene from afar, you might see a man in a crown of thorns as he sought to take the reed unto himself (Mark 15:17). Getting to the reed sometimes resulted in the sheep leader getting wounded (Isaiah 53:5). Can you relate these things to the Good Shepherd? The One injured in hands and feet for you? Christ's stretch to reach you was more extensive and broader than any river (John 3:16). It was longer and more massive than any sin you had committed. He knew where to find the reed among the muck and mirages of a river. The One who entered muddy waters and the blackness of darkness cried, "My God, my God, why hast thou forsaken me?" (Mark 15:34).

Can you relate this to the glorious Shepherd? Can you associate every move of this shepherd with the Great Shepherd of the sheep? How far, how deep, how long was the stretch of Jesus Christ before He reached me and took me to Himself? Only He knows. We were more than waist deep in mud and water when He rescued us. Some were sinking for the third time. Others were immersed in quicksand. There were those whose lifestyle was that of a muddied river, flowing but going nowhere in particular. The shepherd acted as if he had rescued a sheep. He put every effort into his endeavors, just as Jesus did when dying on the cross. If it killed him, if the river swept him off his feet and into the arms of eternity, it didn't matter. He had a passion for reaching a reed, for on the tube he saw its future written.

He Had a Plan before the Action

The shepherd didn't just cut a reed from the side of a pool or river. There were plenty of choices, but to make the reed's choice, he chose it (Ephesians 1:4). He had given plenty of forethought to what he was going to do. As Christ had planned to save you from all eternity (Ephesians 1:4; 1 Peter 1:20), so the shepherd had planned all this as he sat sadly by the smoking embers of the night fire. As he thought on what he was going to do, his mind flared into a flame. The man of sheep even began to draw the shape of the reed in the dust of the floor. As God created Adam from the dust of the earth (Genesis 2:7), so he would make a reed from the dust of his thinking.

From the broken parts of his mind, a thing of beauty and design was formed. He had a plan before the action, which became a plan of action. When he went looking for a reed on which to play his music, he had a plan. Can you believe that from all eternity, God had a plan for your life (Ephesians 1:4)? The reed, as with you, was a designed piece added to piece in a mosaic. The shepherd didn't say, "Then I cast it into the fire, and there came out this calf came" (Exodus 32:24).

The plan doesn't seem to be working sometimes, but that isn't because God has abandoned the plan He has for your life. It is sometimes instead of acting like and being like a reed that we are mere straws in the wind, sometimes wood or stubble. In our rebellious moments, we can become men and women of steel.

We feel we have been growing in mud, wind, and swirling waters for so long. Am I worth saving? Was it worth the effort? God not only "thought so," He "did so." The plan seems to have become a plot to overthrow you. It wouldn't be a plan without pain and effort—not only the action of a hand reaching over a river but a stretch from eternity into time. Sometimes it seems to be going all wrong, without a plan of war or the correct method to save you. That is because you have used your sticky fingers and run them through what the Lord was creating in you. Because of ourselves will we harrow the plan of God, rather than plough according to it.

WE HAVE ALL MADE BAD DECISIONS

This achievement by the Lord is more than face painting or fence painting. It is deep and more profound than any gold mine. He isn't waiting for the paint to dry before He can act. This creation of God is associated with charter and character, Potter and vessel. There have been times when with us all, we have made bad decisions. These decisions have been chipping away at God's arrangements. Remember, for all people say about sin and wrongdoing, they have their consequences. Sin does pay wages. Misconduct does harm people. We aren't of the persuasion that people are drawn into perdition if they love the Lord, but we do believe the ideas that the leader of the sheep had for this reed; blowing in the wind would come to fruition. Those puzzling parts of life would come together, and all would be well.

Note: it was a more excellent and more extensive plan the feeder of sheep had for this reed whistle. Let the great shepherd of the sheep plan it, and you live it!

You will feel that the shepherd's knife cuts you—cuts into the hollow tube, the reed—to separate it from its natural stock. It would be as that grafted into another stock. That knife was the art of the shepherd, as revealed in the slim reed tube, circumcised by the work of the Spirit of God. Our circumcision isn't of the flesh but of the heart (Colossians 2:11; Romans 2:29). When we are born again by the Spirit of the Lord (John 3:6–8), we are removed from the old stock. The veil in our hearts is torn in two to let the darkness out and bring the light. Without severing the flag from its roots, the reed would always have part of the reed nature. What happened to the reed, whose power and ability came from within, was the beginning of a new way of life. What happened to the reed under the knife is what has happened to us, circumcised in heart.

There is a veil across that heart that needs removing through a nail from His cross (2 Corinthians 3:13–16). It needs tearing in two, from top to bottom, and let the tear be because of His tears in Gethsemane (Luke 22:44). Even when we feel that the Lord has torn us apart, when stitched back together again, no one sees where the tear was. We are made whole, one whole new man in Christ (2 Corinthians 5:17). God's triumphs are sometimes in His tears.

THE TOUCH OF CHRIST'S HAND SAVES US

It was the touch of an outstretched hand that transformed the reed into the music coming from a pipe. That hand was empty and yet filled with such fullness of experience, gained throughout the years by the rescuer. The reed had formerly felt the rain, snow, ice, and wind. The sun had shined upon it. The water had touched it as it flowed by, sometimes seeking to rip it apart and sweep it away but with no lasting impression made on it. The reed felt the hand that grasped it. It would lie in that hand until formed into something else. This hand, unlike other indicators, was soft and tender. It handled the cut reed as if it were a newborn lamb.

The reed went from wild nature to the nature of a reed that would produce music. After being touched by the sheep leader's hand, it was changed from one stage of glory to another (2 Corinthians 3:18). It is the hand and arms of Jesus, stretched out on a cross that changes a life for the better. I can't understand the gospel preaching of some who say, "Let the hand touch you, and then if you keep failing God, everything will be all right, because He loves you." That is a false gospel, and such people, whose lives aren't changed, have never felt the touch of the Master's hand. That sort of gospel isn't the hand on the end of the arms, as revealed in Isaiah 53:1.

Your Past, Present, and Future Are in His Hand

The hand that touched the reed is the hand of the Carpenter, Joiner, Healer, Artificer, Potter, and wild-beast Slayer. It was and is as full of grace as the shepherd's hand had been full of sheep's wool during the time of shearing. It is a caring, touching, holding, and shaking hand, changing the reed into something that was to be so different from what it had been.

I daily, even hourly, need to feel the touch of His hand. My past is crushed in that hand; the future of the believer isn't in the palm of their hand. My destiny is in His hand (Hebrews 1:10, 13). That hand takes away the old and brings in the new. The plan for my future living is in that hand, which touched the hollow reed and filled it with music, not the theme of the train going through a tunnel but the music from tender lips, creating me into something and someone who feels the breathings of God in my life.

Four

The Cutting of the
Musical Reed

The shepherd's knife cut into the hollow tube, the reed, to separate it from its natural stock. It is conviction that brings us to Christ (Acts 2:37). It wasn't time for the use of the flat of the blade. Let the water reed see its image in the flat of the blade, but to put to good use, use the sharp cutting edge. That blade must become more than a mirror for a reflection; it must become mighty in its materials. There would be no sable rattling here or leaning on his staff. It wasn't time for counting small flower heads.

The knife would become a tuning blade. The tube must be scarred and scored if it was to be musical and helpful, and if it was to change scenery through the beauty of its music. If the reed were to become anything, it would become something through the cutting blade of a knife. This artist in reed making knew what he was doing and what he wanted to do. One cut too deep, and ruination followed. Another cut not deep enough, or the filter for the rush placed in the wrong area, would result in the reed being cut and collapsing. The blade needed to be handled carefully and usefully. This blade, as conviction and the Word of God, would be far more shaping and tuning than the mud or water ever could. The point of the shepherd's blade had a ministry and mission it would see fulfilled. One would think that to stab anything through the heart would kill it, but not so, for as with conviction, it makes us what He wants us to be (Acts 2:37).

CHRIST DEALS WITH US WITH A GENTLE HAND

The days of the flowing stream and gentle breeze ceased. Sailing boats on rivers on a Sunday afternoon were over the hill and far away, floating, like a straw down the river; they had to stop. There was the call to be something else due to the knife being placed on the pipe. It was like crucifixion, the carving of the cavilling flesh.

The gentle hand, rough through hard work with sheep but soft when it was required, was followed by the point of the blade in the shepherd's hand. That knife was the beginning of the art of the shepherd, as revealed in the slim reed tube. What was the will of the sheep gatherer that would be carved carefully into the reed? He needed the reed, but the reed wasn't sure it needed the shepherd. It was the cutting-edged steel that bridged the gap between shepherd and reed, just as the crook of the shepherd bridged the gap between him and his sheep. This low reed would be made rich and capable through the things it suffered. This was no stabbing attack. The work of the worker wasn't random. It was more like a ransom.

The master of sheep wanted to put his heart into this water flower. What the carpenter will do with the wood or the weaver with wool, so the sheep leader did with the slim tube. The nature of the reed would be kept intact, but a new character, a new plan, would be introduced into it. In that carving was the caring of the artist.

THIS PASTORAL REED BECAME LIKE A "STICK OF JOY"

It was no mean task for the shepherd to transform the empty reed into something that would have the potential for music and dancing. It was a miracle, just as you are a miracle in the making (Psalm

71:7). "Wonder" is "miracle." This pastoral reed became a "stick of joy," since it was reassembled in the hands of the shepherd, having been limited as one would become many in its music ministry into misery. Our shepherd is so kind and gentle that He cuts only where He needs to to leave His mark, however deep the wound, however deep goes the blade, causing it to hurt and wound. There is enough grace to draw together what was severed.

In Jesus Christ, we go from conversion to transformation, then to sanctification and dedication, and then on to consecration. It's in that dedication and consecration that the craftsmanship of the shepherd appeared. What the leader of the flock put into his sheep, he now placed into an empty reed. A hand now operated on this water flag, and that hand became part of it. The reed was being carved and filled with the shepherd's "handiwork," "workmanship," or "masterpiece" (Ephesians 2:10), just as you in your Christian life are supplied by the fullness of God (Ephesians 3:19).

Soon the reed would feel the pricks like a small thorn or the point of a knife digging into it. It is always useless to struggle. If we struggle, it can lead to a muddle. Left as it was, it would accomplish nothing. Torn apart, it would take every part and use it if that tearing came through caring. The rustic pipe was unable to work out what was happening to it. "We know that all things work together for good to them that love God" (Romans 8:28). The "work together" means the "working together" of musical parts until a symphony is produced, using all the discordant sounds of life—the shouts of pain, the grief, the trembling. They are all put together to create praise and worship in the music of your soul. The hurt and pain would soon be made as plain as a plan.

God's Plans Can Include Pain

The pipe produced music in the minor key. It allowed the flute to take its place, enthroned among the trumpet, psaltery, and harp.

It would no longer feel inferior to other flowers of nature or any musical instrument, because of the ability of the one who rescued it put into it. The pain we sometimes endure is that we might enjoy the music of the soul set free. It tunes our hearts, our hearts where the strings become slack, and we go out of tune. The pain and suffering the pipe endured would result in another ministry. Rather than just growing alongside the stream or in marshy land, it would be something more significant than a mountain. No mountain could produce music like this small, thin thing—the last in life, it could mean something.

Others rather than sheep and bears or wandering animals would take notice of it. No longer would it be only a stem of decoration in its proclamation.

That hurt can be the thorn from his crown poking into you to bring you into line and in tune with God. If you get near the throne, expect to feel the hurt from his coronet or crown. It is only allowed that you also may rule and reign in Jesus Christ (Romans 5:17). Let God play the reed, which depicts you and lets what God put into you flow out into the world around. God doesn't always use the same artistic knife to pain us. He has a carvery, and His intention is to use it.

The beam on the face of the finder said it all. The look on the man's face read like an open book. His face was the pattern of joy and delight deeply joined at the hip. There was no requirement here for sunshine. The moonshine, even stars, was diminished by that look of deep satisfaction. It was the sort of satisfaction as if he had gained the world. He was welcoming something into his world that would serve his purposes in music and delight, just as if a man child had been born. Two worlds were intermixed so that the majesty of music might be seen and heard. The man of the sheep could feel a tune already coming into his heart. As he lovingly felt the reed, turning it over and over, he felt like singing.

EVERY SOUND WAS THE SOUND OF MUSIC

The shepherd never heard the scrapings of his knife's blade. Every sound was the sound of music. When the mercy seat was beaten out of one piece of gold, nobody heard a cry for mercy because of the beautiful thing the object was going to offer to others (Exodus 25:17). If the pastoral pipe had been human and had screamed for help, those screams would have fallen on deaf ears. It wasn't killed like a sheep, killed so that it might live—crucified so the life of the shepherd might be seen in it (Galatians 2:20).

Each musical note that sounded from it was one of pain converted into pleasure. Every jarring meant joy; each mark meant music. Within this stick was a paradise of pleasure as many listened to its music. The crestfallen and the forlorn felt that life reformulated. Number 26 would become number 1.

Ears that are part of working out a plan for a life hear no whimpers or screams. Here was a man seeking to bring music out of cymbals, and that isn't an easy task. It is terrific when we speak of anyone playing a musical instrument; we refer to them as "playing" that instrument. It must be tuned before it can be taken and trusted. The turning and spinning it endured as the hand became a lathe was nonstop. If it was held captive for a while, it was only to be released into something far more significant. Placed into the pipe would be the "Song of the Soul Set Free." He looked like a fisherman who had just been fishing and had caught the catch of the day. Here was the center forward who had scored the winning goal. His pleasure was in the measure of his carving the rush.

WE NEED OUR HEARTS TO BE CIRCUMCISED

The glory of the shepherd became the glory of the flag. What the shepherd did reminds us of was the fact that the moment the hand of our shepherd came upon us, we were circumcised—not with a knife or through human hands but by the work of the Spirit of God. Our circumcision isn't of the flesh but of the heart (Colossians 2:11; Romans 2:29). When we are born again by the Spirit of the Lord (John 3:7), we are removed from the old stock. The reed would always have part of the reed of nature.

As a believer, in the future, it would be part of two natures. The shepherd had to make it so the old nature didn't dominate the new. The opening up of the stick didn't look pretty—cut, carved, and centered in music. It had to realize that even though there was a release of this new nature, it would never be of any use unless it yielded to the hands and will of its rescuer and restorer.

The knife, as a king, presented to it a new nature. It must bow to what he had decided for it. There wasn't a need to dress it up in a party frock or to put on a long, white gown. It had to play. The pain it suffered had released in its music. Its ability had to be seen, heard, and loved to be understood.

The difference was, instead of blowing wind on it and making truly little noise, it now had the breath of the shepherd, and from it sounded out not just a racket of blowing in the wind. What happened to the pastoral reed was the beginning of a new way of life. What happened to the reed under the knife of the shepherd is what has happened to us by being circumcised in heart.

THE HAND OF GOD IS A GREAT TEACHER AND LEADER

It took place in His hand, a hand large enough to crush despair and put something to greater use. It was this same hand that would stop destroying insects from attacking the reed without notice or favor. A hand was soft and gentle enough to cover during the time of restless storms. That hand became a cover in a time of storm. It became a university for the reed. It was the hand that lifted it and loved the hollow thing as He lifted it to His breast.

It must now work to good use. One of the first things the reed seeker did was put the reed to his mouth to test its strength and ability. Was it hollow enough? Was it small enough? Could it be used for the purpose it was designed for? Could he trust it? Would it be worth the effort of seeking and finding it like a lost sheep? This is like us in conversion. It was taken from one environment and put into another (Colossians 1:13), taken from one world and placed into another. A world of uncertainty, the certainty of the world of the music lover's. It was lifted from the water and brought close to the shepherd. It is what Christ does when He rescues us; the stalk was rescued from the ebb and flow of the river. That help became the bridge that brought it into use. In the sheep lover's times of tiredness and sickness, feeling that he couldn't go on while on the verge of letting sheep leadership slip away from him, the music stick would become the bandmaster. It could be his soothing toy, better than a bottle of herbs or a leaf applied to a wound.

The Shepherd Loved the Reed He Chose

The shepherd loved the reed he chose—"love" meaning "strong liking and affection." It wasn't the emotion some use when naming love. If I kept telling you that the shepherd loved the reed and nothing else, eventually you would get tired of my harping with broken harp strings, and I would become the proverbial broken record. You would want to know, is there something more to the shepherd than him just loving that reed, which was to become his stick of music?

God Isn't Only Love

Was that the beginning and end of the shepherd's ministry? Just music, music, music? A great ministry indeed, but this reed taker and maker was also a shepherd. Anyone would tell you that an eastern shepherd is like our farmers—men and women of multiple abilities, of dexterity, whether driving a tractor, sowing seed, harvesting, being a mechanic, or doing a multitude of other things crammed into one man. The answer would be, of course, that there is more than one aspect to this shepherd. He isn't only one thing. He is many things, but he is also almost all things to all men, just as our Great Shepherd is.

What about the shepherd's crook used to rescue sheep? That rod was special because notches were cut into it every time a wild animal was overcome. That rod was stained with blood, like the cross we believe, was a stained cross. What about his stone and sling, which he used to beat off the wild animals? Tell me about his clothing, made from the skins of the slain, made from marauding animals, which lived again in the actions of the sheep lover. What about the anointing oil, required for healing? What about the knife he used to pare the reed? Friend, there is more to God, Jesus Christ, the Great Shepherd of the sheep than love! (Hebrews 13:20). Love is His nature, but from that springs many attributes. God's primary characteristic may be water, but from His throne, from that water, are many created streams, fountains, and lakes (Ezekiel 47:4–5.6–7).

LOVE BECOMES MANY THINGS

God has a whole armory, not just a sword (Ephesians 6:11–17). If an artist had to keep drawing or painting mankind with only one leg and no eyes, ears, mouth, feet, or hands, you would think it was a misrepresentation of mankind. The same applies to the love of God. We try to emphasize His love at the expense of what our love should be for Him. That love is His nature, and it isn't mere human emotion or sentiment. God has many other aspects of His life.

There were many sides to God, just as there are of any diamond. Even the knife blade had four sides. Two are flat and dull; the other two are as sharp as a pain. The knife you hold in your palm can cut and hurt; it can also sever ropes and set something free. It can, as a knife, butter or cool a bee sting with its cold blade. It can help you in eating by cutting that meal into mouth-sized portions. Again, if I only ever mentioned the judgment of the Lord or the holiness of God, and that was all, you would get fed up with it. What about talking about His wrath? I would be conveying only part of the truth.

Think and thank God for the many uses of His love. Think of the benefits of the shepherd's staff or rod. Lean on it, yes. That isn't its only office. It helped to rescue sheep. The tip of it can count the sheep as they are dipped. The bottom of it can be used to stir up the fire (2 Timothy 1:6), to "rekindle." Within the shepherd's crook were several compartments. In one was oil; in another there was a piece of bread. There might be a rude compass in another screwed container of the staff. There would undoubtedly be a flint for fire starting. He wouldn't always be rubbing two sticks together to create a blaze.

THIS GOD AND FATHER OF OURS

Your shepherd is both heaven and hell, righteousness and peace, mercy and grace (1 Timothy 1:2). This God and Father of ours, who is love, is also wrathful. He can be jealous (Numbers 25:11). He can be vengeful. He is a God of wrath. He is merciful, kind, and generous, but I mustn't lose sight of the full revelation of God in Jesus Christ, who drove people out of the temple (John 2:15). Who called people a viper's brood. Who said it would be more tolerable for Sodom and Gomorrah than for them in the day of judgment? He called hypocrites "whitewashed tombs" (Luke 11:47–48; Matthew 23:27).

If others were describing the creation and all they ever mentioned was the sun, you would get tired of that. The botanist, agriculturist, naturalist, ornithologist, and scientist would proclaim that there is more to creation than the sun. There are the earth, trees, flowers, mountains, oceans, and forests—to name only a few of its splendors.

Terry Atkinson

By overemphasizing one thing, as some do, with the love of God, they have weakened the rest. We do God an injustice by proclaiming only one aspect of His divine nature.

Tell others about His love and tell them He is a God of grace coupled with judgment. Do not portray a God who is made up of only love. Give us "the truth, the whole truth and nothing but the truth" (taken from an English courtroom oath). Do not keep preaching a one-sided, lopsided God. Please give us and believe in the whole counsel of God. Tell me about all His features and don't miss out on His other attributes at the expense of "over-egging" the one thing: love. To keep the music sweet and balanced, we need the truth, the whole truth, and nothing but the truth. To play that instrument, we need all the scales, not just one note. One song played for all occasions would be so predictable and boring.

Five

The Piercing and Shaping of the Musical Reed

The moment arrived! The reed was rescued from swirling waters. There was no possibility of it being taken away; it was anchored in a hand that would never let it go. Often it would feel the warm imprint of that hand on its face. The lines there would line the reed with comfort. Every line was a path. Every mark on that hand was a mark of redemption. It wasn't taken to be creative but to have its usefulness more than simply stated but declared through music. That hand would drown out any noisome beats or unpleasant sounds. The flute, like you, would always in the future have a cover during the time of storm. As every ship has its harbor, this music measure would have one in the hand that lifted it. It would never need to compete with anybody else because the music stick was the competition. The competition was complete because it was complete in him who had graced it with his work and would play the strings of his heart through it. It would always win "hands down," his "hands" that held it.

Terry Atkinson

GOD SEEKS TO ALLAY YOUR FEARS

The word and work of the sheep keeper were to bring security to the flag. Now it had little fear of being broken by wind or clawed by a bird of prey. The shepherd's steps were those of the musical instrument. It would never be a loud, blasting trumpet or a foghorn. It needed to be only what destiny had decided. There were hidden treasures in it, about to be revealed. There were splendid qualities that would ring the rafters through its many tunes, tunes of hope and not fear, melodies of joy and mercy. The emotions of the shepherd are stirred and dance hand in hand as it taken brought from defeat to triumph.

It would now be taken from where it had been found into many different areas, as the shepherd led the sheep from pasture to pasture, into dark caves, that it knew nothing. In those dark caves, it would be the only light in "light" music. It wouldn't be a journey or a destination of self-help or effort. Carried along like a baby in arms, secure and settled, it would never need to make choices because the choice had been made for it. One thing, weak and unusable, would be changed—not in a moment or the twinkling of an eye but through the process of pain and endurance.

GRACE BRINGS VARIETY TO LIFE

It had been to only one scene in life, and that was the picture of water as it flowed by it. What had been just the pictures of fallen leaves and drifting wood would be no more. It was taken, and many things would be added to it. The hollow tube wouldn't come through natural growth, but something would be added carefully to turn that useless thing into something useful. The stalk would be better than being lost and found. What was taken from it? What was taken from its life, as it surrendered to the knife of the hillside farmer, would be missed. If it had many dreams, each dream would be fulfilled, the will and desires of another poured through it in another form.

What had been just a small stream or trickle of water would become a cataract of music. The tube of music would be taken from one valley to another, knowing that the good thing about any valley was that it would lead to a mountain and a beautiful view. It would help another as he climbed. It would never dip with the valley, but it would always be the same yesterday, today, and tomorrow. We must be prepared as believers to be carried along, and as we are borne along, we need to be prepared to be used in every circumstance. As Christians, we must stop struggling, kicking, and screaming against what our shepherd, seen in the face of the Father, wants to do for us and in us (John 14:8). The word *suffice* means "satisfaction" or having more than enough. The best advice, and the thing that brings any child being born along, is "settle into surrender." Take the Scouts motto: "Be prepared!" (the motto used by the Scouts worldwide).

Your Security Becomes Your Serenity

It was from this moment, that is, through yielding and obedience, that the bruised reed would be carried "in," "by," and "through" grace from one mountain to another. No pebble in the way would halt its progress. No barrier would be too great to be leaped over, because of the one carrying it. Away from a stagnant pool or marshy pond, led from fountain to fountain, it would be taken from fountain to mountain. The musical reed's strength was the strength of the shepherd. He was no blade of grass blown hither and thither. It would send its musical ability through tender grasses and by still waters (Psalm 23:2). It would know its highs and lows, but it would always be in the clothing or hand of the shepherd. Its serenity was in his security. It was taken through flood, storm, hot, and cold day. The changing scenes of weather or changing moods wouldn't change what had been changed into something beautiful from what was only plain and ugly.

That shielding hand, the hand of Christ, saved it in every situation (Psalm 31:15). It felt to the stalk when that problem became more extensive and the burden became heavier, as if nothing had changed, simply because the hand that carried it and played it and taught it to sound out music was never weak. This was because when things changed, the hand holding it never changed (Malachi 3:6). This meant that, like you, Christian, it didn't have to cling on. Its future was safe with the seven marks on the shepherd's palm. There was peace in that palm, as there is in the hands of the One who said, "Peace, be still!" (Mark 4:39).

As the sheep leader battled with a marauding beast, the reed knew it was secure in him. It was saved from drowning in the very waters it had been plucked from. No wind would blow it away. The security it lacked as it grew in the marshy land was now in what it was placed in. This reed felt stronger than steel because of the power of the one who owned it, loved it, carved it, and sealed it with his lips. This music tube wouldn't crumble into dust. It feared no hard stone or rock. It could "do all things" through the hand that carried it (1 Peter 5:10). One word used for "strengthening," found in 2 Chronicles 12:1, means "harness." Our durability comes through Christ's ability. It was covered so that the hot midday sun didn't bake or harden it until it was unpliable. It was kept from going out of tune. The master musician was always there to retune it, making the next sound better than the one before it. Without many purposes, it had found a drive in a shepherd who cared enough to call and collect it.

WE ALL EXPERIENCE GOOD AND BAD DAYS

Before it lay good and bad days, days of sunshine; and the blackest of night would be animated by its music. On the blackest of nights, it could be a shining star. You can't measure a bad or good day through your emotions. As this cut reed rested in the hand and clothing of the sheep shearer, we must rest in the hand of the Lord. Each must be taken hold of and used. If it is a bad day, learn to brighten it with the music of your character. What you "are," what you "do," or what is "seen" in you is your music. There would be no "darkest before the dawn," for the reed would always be in the light of its musical ability.

Planted in the plan were plans of usefulness and not pain. In the collecting of it would be found diversity in the unity of the hand. Because it belonged to one, it was able to bless many. If it belonged to many, it would bless none. "Whose I am and whom I serve" (Acts 27:23). It was as useful to the Hebrew soldier or Roman guard as a quiver full of arrows. We all want to be an Onesimus, meaning "useful" or "profitable" (Philemon 10).

Even in adversity, it would know diversity. It would never have to throw back what was thrown at it. It could answer everything in music. Any entanglement could be resolved by song. There would be no bare days before it. In these areas, it was still expected to let its heart hang out in its music. This could be a time of rest or resistance. Be a Christian; be part of the Lord wherever you go, and in whatever happens to you, learn to trust Him at "all times"—good, bad, dark, and light (Proverbs 3:5). "When in Rome, do as Christians would do." Be what God has made you. Don't try to be the shepherd. Don't try to be what you are not. The pipe would always have its limitations, but the hand that held it would never be limited.

Remember, He is Father, and you are a believer. Learn to trust Him when all the lights go out. It was Paul and Silas who sang at midnight (Acts 16:25). It was being taken, and a mere reed was tuned through conversion into an organ. All the reed had to do was trust the shepherd in high or deep, low, or only a stream. Learning to trust the Almighty in the good armors you to meet with the bad and turn it into a blessing. The reed didn't need to hide in any corner while it was in his hand. That hand brought the stability needed; it wasn't a see-saw experience. In these situations, as the reed leaned near his breast, it would be carried from one place to another. Its passage through everything was free with grace, gratis.

Something So Small Could Be a Blessing

There was a ministry, a gift in the tube, that would be revealed. Who would have thought that something so small could be such a blessing? Can you use your imagination? There is an imaginary story we tell the children in Sunday school class. The cedar tree from Lebanon was cut down. From its wood came the boat Jesus fished from. Then a cross was made from the same wood, on which they crucified our Lord. Later, a barrel was made, and a young lad hid in it and discovered a plot to kill the apostle Paul (Acts 23:16).

When hills, mountains, and valleys failed to meet the deep longing in the heart of the pastoral man, the pipe was there to suffice. The sheep wouldn't be used to get the shepherd a deep sleep. He couldn't sleep some nights, so he took out his favorite, soothing stick, and it worked wonders. No sooner had he begun to play than the troubled feeder and seeker of sheep quietly and quickly by the firelight fell asleep. It had become a wall of peace, and into that peace, he entered.

It had a ministry deeper than any well. It could outrace any river as music poured from it. Here was a fountain in a desert. It reached where other things couldn't get. It had the ability to climb into the shepherd's heart and restore his smile. It could convert any pang of pain into the melody of the moment.

When all around were parched, water music came from the water stick. It could turn morning into noonday, mourning into dancing. It was that overflowing cup David described in Psalm 23:5. Turning and creating night into a beautiful sight, it had that sort of charm that could turn that dry and dusty place into a well-watered plot of land, an oasis in the desert. When everything went wrong that could go wrong, this was always right; it always knew its place and would always give of its best in the worse situation, describing what every Christian longs to do and be in the hands of Christ.

The Reed Brought Rejoicing

A sheep was missing, so the leader's calculations told him. Where had it fallen? Where had he been? These and many more epithets went through the mind of the carer as wind raced through the corn. Why hadn't he heard its cry? If a lamb had been taken, out came the pipe reed, which was used to signal his thankfulness when a sheep was found (Luke 15:5). This was better than the best food, for it was the food of deep desire. It kindled strong liking and affection. It was the only stick required to light the fire of passion. Hunger could be enlarged as the flute was played. This reed was his banquet and stick of joy or "joystick." With the reed held securely, the cup of the shepherd was always full and overflowing.

The reed was created for these moments. It was its gift that turned gory into the glory. It was at bad times that it was used to produce good things, things that would linger in the spirit of all who heard for many days, months, and years. Its music remained long in the shadows in the man's heart. If he had no other friend, he would always have one in the flag. He could call on it as any time, for it was as a faithful servant. It was the man of his right hand. It was able to put fresh hope into the heart.

This was better than a lantern or candle lit on a dark, dreary night. On a stormy day, this was his rainbow. It lightened dead feet. It lifted the hands that hung down and strengthened feeble knees (Hebrews 12:12). The words that described its work were "Here I am, wholly available, as for me and my house we will serve the Lord" (Isaiah 6:8; Romans 12:1). Some will put their shoulder to the wheel, but the reed put its music to far better use and accomplished more.

Terry Atkinson

You Will Never Understand All Things

It was the pipe tube that could bring out the best in both sheep and shepherd. When it was played, the sheep seemed to be more obedient to follow his leadership. Learn to "be" your best in the worst possible situation, and when you have good, then "do" your best. If someone falls and bruises their leg, the sun doesn't stop shining. If some people lose faith, the sun won't cease to shine. If there are things you don't understand, keep on being a piece of sweet music coming from a pastoral stick. Stick with it!

Music has charms. This stick had such "charms" coming from a Latin word, meaning "music." Its greatest moments were our greatest moments when we felt that we were in the hands of our shepherd and could do all things through Christ who strengthens us (Philippians 4:13). The power lies within you to redraw terrible situations into moments of deep love and great pleasure. Through your converted spirit, you can see flowers growing out of wounds. That is a ministry worth having!

All This Pain Was Part of a Plan

It was between these journeys that the glory of the shepherd would be revealed through the musical tube. Let music become your full stops in life. It had to have marks added to it. This meant that in the hands of the sheep lover, there was deep penetration into the tube. Things happened to it that would hurt. All this pain was part of the leader of sheep's choice. It would produce music, music that went up and down scales, used in the heights and depths of life to help and nurture us. It was music that was far more worthy of being in a place and heard by a king than of being in a puddle of mud and being listened to by bleating sheep. What a contrast! The sound of music was from the pipe, and the noise was coming from the sheep.

CONVERTED INTO A MUSICAL BOX OF GREAT POTENTIAL

What might have been just a hollow coffin had been converted into a musical box of great potential. It could have been only a stick, used to draw plans in the sand. It wasn't the size, length, or the strength of the tube that made the music; it was the shepherd. Learn that in your conversion; it isn't what you can do, but what will you let the shepherd do to and through you? The emptier and hollower it was, the sweeter the music. It was so great because in it there was little resistance to musical notes. Let the glory of God shine through you as the music sounds from this tube.

The most warming thing on a cold day or night, winter or summer, was to feel the warm lips and hot breath of the shepherd on it, as he sought to play a merry tune and set the dark, dank hills alive with the sound of music. Being used meant it was suitable and usable. There was no other musical reed like this one; it stood as a Mount Everest in its achievements through the shepherd. The only limitations to your life are you. Poor workers blame their tools. Good workhorses get on with the job before them. Don't complain that the door is locked if you have the key.

There was such a repertoire of music production from the tube, since there were so many aspects of Christianity. There would be tunes of deep feeling, themes and songs of the merry. Music fit for a feast and a priest. Songs and psalms will always develop free moments from, sometimes the position of strangulation.

Songs were composed of everyday happenings, which would be played through this hollow reed. The sheep gatherer was adept at taking hurts and pain, and transposing them into music. What had gone wrong the day before was now put to music, and it didn't seem half as bad when played or sung using a musical instrument. Whatever mood the carer of lambs was in, that was expressed through the empty tube. He filled what was empty. When he played it, it was more than the sound of a train passing through a tunnel. It was as music from the heavens, which was required to be interpreted on earth.

Terry Atkinson

FROM THE TUBE CAME GREAT REJOICING

Can you see it? Can you hear the pipe played as all sheep pass safely through the swelling torrent? Is it this tube that angels play when one sinner repents, which Jesus spoke of (Luke 15:10)? Was it something like this reed that angels used at the birth of Christ (Luke 2:13)? More than a song of rejoicing came from it; it was the song of an army returning with great spoil, rejoicing through the reed, more than the time of wine or harvest. Sometimes trumpets are blown when the king returns from abdication. It was the triumphant music played each time the sheep passed through a river or stream. Instead of feeling the teeth of the marauder, the rescued lamb heard the sweet songs of serenades through a hollow tube as the tender lips of the shepherd were placed around the reed.

You could march to this music. It presented no dirge, as at a funeral. When the river flowed low, this musical reed brought it back to its proper level. When a river was difficult to ford, a bridge of music bridged the depth as they all passed over safely. Birds that had ceased to sing sang again as the songs of the winged came forth.

When the shepherd played music through the tube and you used your imagination, you could see armies coming over the hills to their rescue. Here came the cavalry! Scenes and shouts could be converted by the sounds coming from the reed. Weddings or funeral sounds could be heard coming from the cut reed. So modest, so empty, and yet so full and accomplished as our lives should be in Jesus Christ.

In the deep winter, the reed could melt the frosts. It could see spring arrive early. Every day and in every way, it could be a summer's day. In the autumn of any life, it could bring the joy of birth. When leaves faded and were read to fall, this musical instrument got them back to life again. You would never grow old or weary since you were captivated by its contents. When the road ended, it commenced also as reed music was heard. What would have been a sheer drop and certain death was avoided through the message of music as it was played. Life was so different now because it had found its "pitch" in the music sent forth from it as an ambassador.

Six

The Christian Experiences in the Musical Reed

T here is such an abundance of waters in which the shepherd can dip the soiled reed. Sometimes those waters are turbulent. On other occasions, they go softly as the waters of Shiloah (Isaiah 8:6). There will be different experiences you come through, but always remember that the hand that placed you in the waters—be they soft, silent, or stormy waters—is the same one that will lift you back out as He brings you through. The swelling waters that would sweep you away will pass over and through the Shepherd's fingers.

The safest place in the world for you or the pipe with rod and staff, stone and sling, is in the palm of His hand. You can then become His handyman in all things. Where He hesitates to go, when it is too difficult to enter some crises, He will send music through you to bring change where there is decay. The depth of the waters doesn't count with Christ. They could measure a "fathom," meaning the distance between "two outstretched arms," those arms stretched from heaven to earth to save you. Every reach is within His reach.

Experiences in the Lord are as varied and as many as streams, rivers, seas, and oceans. The same element, water, is in each of these, but the depth, as with life's experiences, is different. He stands and waits as a lifeguard as you enter uncharted waters. What you know about wind, waves, or storms, He has forgotten. Your God, who created the waters of the oceans of the world, is also the God who created the tear duct, the tear, and sweat. The shepherd didn't allow any sheep or lamb to drown. He tested the water before he let the sheep enter it. The shepherd who carried the pipe also brought a lamb on his shoulders before others could enter. No matter how deep you sink, you will never drop to the place called hell.

LIVE YOUR LIFE AS A SYMPHONY OF WORSHIP

The life you live for Christ can be as music, which was the shepherd's ambassador. When you heard music in the valley, you knew the shepherd would soon appear. So live in such a way that people will want to dance to your tune. Have such a wonderful life that it will sweep people off their feet and into the arms of an awaiting Jesus Christ (Matthew 11:28).

One thing contains such healing balm, the grace of God, sounding out as the Word of God "sounded out" from the Thessalonian church (1 Thessalonians 1:8). They became a sounding board for music. That music can bring the best out of those whose hearts are discordant and need retuning. Broken heartstrings that have been pulled until they are broken can be healed. Slumbering cords can be reawakened. The craft, just like this music tube, which carries Christ, arrives at the other side (Mark 4:36; 5:1). It won't sink on the brink. It will receive the blessing that floats the boat.

GO DEEPER AND DEEPER INTO THE WORD

The great Shepherd of the sheep will lead you into the water of the Word (Ephesians 5:26). If He does, don't just be dunked. Christ through His word will make sure these aren't waters to put your toe into or to swim in; but they are waters in which we must trust in Him when passing through. Deep waters will never wash the music out of the right tube of music. Not a sprinkling but a baptism! If you are going for God, go for gold. Don't make a small splash; take a dive into the deep. Go where whales can't go. Go to new depths in your experience, assisted by the music that comes through His orchestral Word (Romans 8:28). "Work together" meaning "symphony." Your sweet, unrivalled music will come when your "pitch" is in the word of the Almighty. The swallow skims the surface.

Learn to swim in the lake of love. The breaststroke, that feeling of compassion, is a good start. Don't be as a floating leaf on the surface. In experience, let others play a dirge; you play marching music, the marching music of Zion. Let some "light music" stream through you like beams of sunshine. Learn through your enrichment to make people feel good. The Word of God is the music that opens many doors into the heart. That is why Acts 16:26 says, "All the doors were opened" after Paul and Silas had sung the first Pentecostal duet. While and when you are passing through any experience, never limit yourself to coming and going. Come and meditate in the Bible, and many buoys found in it. There are warnings there of people who have made shipwreck of their faith (1 Timothy 1:19). If you want to realize how deep or shallow you are in His Word, measure yourself not by another's music book but by God's. The Bible is no desert island. It is occupied, and many are its adherents. It has a full crew, who are always ready to rescue and bring us closer to the Lord.

Always believe in the hand from above, which holds you and has charmed you by its grace. Grace is your goal, and you will be a winner. There are waters to swim in. Leave the beach behind. Seek horizons that are far away. Lose sight of the shores of your own ability. Go where there are no perimeters into deep depths. Be as those who go down to the sea and see the wonderful works of God (Psalm 77:19).

Terry Atkinson

LAUNCH OUT INTO THE DEEP

Whenever you come to the Bible, don't just go in there at toe depth. Launch out into the deep. Many criticized Peter when he stepped out of the boat, but at least he went over the side to follow Jesus (Matthew 14:28–31). He had decided that if "He is going along the sea surface, I must go there too." There is no feeling better than riding on a board on the crest of a wave, coming into the depths of the fountains of the deep broken up (Genesis 7:11). Come to the waters of the Word with an empty chalice and see your cup full and running over (Psalm 23:5). Those who feel like fainting need the waters you collect, water turned into wine (John 2:1–11).

Go deeper and deeper until, as in the book of Ezekiel, you have waters up to your loins, then waters to swim in (Ezekiel 47:5). Is it too much to ask that when you come to meditate, come as a fish into waters and find your national and natural identity? It is into the waters of the depths of the Bible that we need to come. The reed came to these waters. If the pastoral pipe went back into the waters it came from, it was that it might be washed and sanctified. The depths of the Bible won't destroy your potential or your music. It will produce a clean pipe ready for the pure hand of the Master musician. You will be that vessel, created and fit for the Master's use (2 Timothy 2:21). Ask the eternal God to widen your capacity. The reed didn't stay with one note or tube, one song or one lilt. Go into the abundance of the Word of God and come from it fruitful as a vine in season.

We need more than one type of water. The waters of a storm can still work miracles in us as we come to the Word of God as a type of water. There are times when we need the gold and other rare jewels from the rivers that flowed from the garden of Eden (Genesis 2:10–14). There are moments when we need to come through the hand of our shepherd into the calm waters of Psalm 23:2, "waters of quietness," with pastures of tenderness.

The Abundance That Is in the Word of God

There is a need when we want to rejoice and shout aloud, to be dipped or to come to read and experience the cup that is full and overflowing (Psalm 23:5). The abundance that is in the Word of God is described when it says, "Now the Jordan was in full flood" (Joshua 3:15). It is when our souls thirst for God that we come to the Word and long for a drink to slake our thirst from the water of the well in Bethlehem (2 Samuel 23:15). King David wanted water from that well, because it spoke of first love. It was where he had played as a boy. Yet for all his achievements, he wanted to pour them out at God's feet. David wanted everything baptized in first love for Jehovah.

Washing of Water by the Word

Holy writ calls it "washing of water by the word" (Ephesians 5:26). There will be times when bowed down, and even on all fours, we crawl to the Word of God for help and strength. When you open your Bible, you open a flower filled with nectar. There are times when we feel dragged through the mud. It is then that we require the "washing of water, through the Word" (Ephesians 5:26). The Word that we come to, and sometimes dip into, will be the means of opening a new continent of character and experience to you as a believer. When you read this Word, it reads you. You know we have margins in some Bibles, and we place comments in those margins. It's the washing we receive through the Word that reaches into the margins of our lives.

He Needs to Keep It Clean and Unblocked

Things we don't see as essential will enhance our ability to play music. How often have you seen the instrument player wiping the tube's end of his instrument? He wants to; he needs to keep it clean and unblocked, so the music won't be distorted as some radio barely on its station point. You won't have to row your boat in these waters. You will meet with Jesus who walked on water. It becomes your springboard into another new day. On each occasion, when you open your Bible, you open a door into the vast expanse of what God is. Oceans of His love come flooding in. It makes you realize that when John Baptist baptized converts, he went where there was much water (John 3:23). The moment they were saved, they wanted to go deeper. This reed needed to learn more and more, and it did through the music that poured through it like water. This wasn't the reed falling into water. It was taken there so it might be cleansed.

Be Cleansed through the Word

When the shepherd took the reed pipe and dipped it into flowing waters, he sustained and prolonged the life of the stick that was to produce music. In His word is eternal life (John 5:39). Dig deep and find buried treasure. The pipe requires the washing in water to allow the music to flow through it. Washing through the water made way for the music to flow. The music then followed the flow of the stream. This meant it wouldn't lose its resonance. It needed to be clean and supple. This reed was to be holy.

You will always come to the Word when you are dry, for it is a bottomless reservoir. That Word needs to flow over you and through you as the water flowed over and through the flute. If the pipe became misshaped, it needed dipping into water, as we are required to come to the Word of God. Some pearls lose their color, but if plunged into seawater, their color is restored. The Word of God has therapeutic qualities. It tunes our hearts to say and sing His praise. If the pipe of music was difficult to handle, the answer was found in the water, the Word, where it found a new shape. If its music seemed to be dull, as dull as dishwater, it required another visit to the spring of life. When it appeared to have lost its ability and was out of tune, the tuning fork was the water. The Word of God to us is what the water was to the shepherd's reed.

The Experience of the Reed Is Your Story

The experience of the bruised reed is your story, a story that makes experience write something in the center of your being. All that was happening to the reed will happen to you, expressing the glory of the shepherd. The pipe was constructed as more than a "blowpipe." No poisonous dart was flung from it. No hot air was flowing through this vehicle, only the breath of the sheep shearer. The stem was no peashooter we used as children. What you have passed through—are passing through without passing out—won't be washed away, no matter how deep or intense the water. Some things happen to us as believers. It seems as if life is scribed with a pen of iron. Don't let it be a pen of iron trying to scribe a piece of rock. Let your heart be as a writing pad, where the clay was soft and yielding. There is some rocky part of our character the Lord needs to use a chisel on. He will chisel into the rock.

When writing about the suffering and bruising of the pipe reed, I don't mean anyone who deliberately keeps walking in sin and pretends to love God. We believe in the surer foundation and experience than those who sin against the Word of God. Some are so deaf as a doorpost. Even worse, there are none so deaf as those who don't want to listen. We have taken the cloth of this world and stuffed our ears with it. We, like those in the book of Hebrews, have become "dull of hearing" (Hebrews 5:11). We have wax in our ears that require washing out. We can become as silent as the grave, as unyielding as a stone tear, when we hear a voice saying, "This is the way, walk ye in it" (Isaiah 30:21).

Terry Atkinson

TAKE UP THE POSITION OF THE BRUISED REED

Being a bruised reed doesn't include those who are foolhardy and want their way. I do mean those devoted Christians who fall on hard times when everything seems to go wrong. When there is an illness or a death in the family, when you lose your employment, you then take up the position of the bruised reed, since you feel crushed. The text (Matthew 12:20) refers to those who feel like they have gone beyond the trickle of water or light rain; heavy rain has come down, and the floods have come up. Isaiah 42:3 mentions the fact that coming Christ wouldn't "brush aside the bruised and the hurt." "He won't disregard the small and insignificant." This attitude and spirit are a world away from this world.

THE REED BELONGED TO THE SHEPHERD

There will be months, days, and years when "cross bearing" is denying yourself for Christ. The difficult part of cross bearing is that it is daily. Daily I must pray. Every day I must meditate. Daily I must witness for my Lord. The work can be so hard. Living for Jesus can be and will be as tricky as trying to write with a pen by using the end that has no nib or ink. The reed belonged to the shepherd. There was a deepening relationship between them that was enhanced by its music. If you are in doubt, turn to the Word of God for the washing away of doubt and the bringing in of assurance. That Word, like water, will wash away all the doubt and rebellion if you are dipped deep enough. The sheep knew all about "dipping"; it marked out to whom they belonged. "Whose I am and whom I serve" (Acts 27:23). The Word turns you into a convert; you become something you never thought you would be. "Ye are not your own, you are bought with a price" (1 Corinthians 6:20).

Trying to Write a Love Letter with Your Finger

When you are being misunderstood, it can be worse than that, and it can be like trying to write a love letter with your little finger. There are times when everything seems to have come from a jumble sale into your life. You are like books scattered on the floor that need to be placed alphabetically on a shelf. The Word has the power to do this, since the Word, Jesus Christ as Shepherd, can arrange music in your heart. The secret of not being "off-key" is to make Christ the "key" to every closed door presented to you.

Stop complaining that the door is shut. You have the bunch of keys hanging around your middle instead of in your heart. Let that music coming from you be of His composition, and if it is, you will have His disposition. This is music that is composed for you, for each occasion. There are moments when you, as a person who obeys the Word of the Lord, will feel that you are rowing against the tide. For some people with such an experience, there is always help in God. Read the Word! Be that Word you have read, and if you do, you will go on to sound out music as you live from the music book, the Bible.

Let "water from the Word" wash away all your fear and fumbling. Be God's musical reed, and if you do, you will exercise far more influence than the Pied Piper of Hamelin, who could play music so sweet that rats came from every hole dislodged from a town. (The Pipe Piper is part of a German legend. He was known as Pan Piper or Pan Rat Catcher. Through his beautiful music, he emptied the town of Hamelin, Germany, of rats. When the citizens refused to pay him, he played such lovely music that the children followed him.) There is power in the music that will come from the bruised reed. What the Lord puts into you can be so wonderful, since it *is* powerful. You will become majestic if through His Word you discover His majesty.

Seven

The Christian Doctrines in the Musical Reed

Step by step, day by day, hour by hour, your life is lived out in the experience of the shepherd's music reed. The leader and feeder of lambs traveled many scenic routes and pathways leading to pleasure. No one experience could cover the "paths of righteousness," as found in Psalm 23:3. These, because of your Guide, are "right paths," which lead to wholesome experiences in God.

The Christian life will always be like the opening of a flower's petals. There is nectar here developed into honey. It isn't just the color, stamens, or the stems; the petals are positioned in a way that makes the flower into an exceptional beauty. It is the bulb, hidden below the surface, that will determine its beauty and how much it is appreciated. There is what is produced by a new nature, and to help us, God has placed doctrines, the way to act, think, and speak, in His Word. The doctrines of the Word are the "marks" of the high calling that is ours. "I press toward the mark for the prize of the high calling of God in Christ Jesus," I press "within the marks" toward the high calling of God (Philippians 3:14). What we believe makes us what we are. It must be "wholesome" doctrine. The word *wholesome* is a medical term meaning "healthy." "Wholesome" doctrine can describe a ship with a full crew (1 Timothy 6:3).

We must "adorn" the doctrine of God (Titus 2:10). The word describes a bride in her wedding dress. The word *adorn*, used in Titus 2:10, means like an ornament placed on a shelf or as a picture put onto a wall; these "adorn" where they are, and we must, as bruised reeds, do the same.

These truths apply to Christian doctrine. We need the truth, the whole truth of Bible truth, that will take us into different pastures after traveling along many paths of peace. Always bring to your memory that error is a zigzag line, while the truth is a straight line.

The next step for the reed was that of sanctification, developed through the Word of God (1 Thessalonians 5:23). Once we have been in the hands of the Great Shepherd, we too will become sanctified. It was those hands that set the reed apart for only one purpose—not created to be the rod, staff, stone, or sling but to be a reed, held close to its creator. It was plucked from the riverside or the side of a pond to be with the sheep's guide and tubes musician. You are saved and sanctified to be with Him (Mark 3:13).

When those hands are placed around us, as the sheep keeper's hands around the cut reed, we will enter the experience of being set apart for God. The Queen of England has a particular sword. It is with this sword that she knights people of the realm. That sword is sanctified, because it is set apart, wherever it is, with one sole purpose of being used in one particular way—not used to fight battles or to kill people. The "sword of ceremony" is so mighty when being used by the owner, distinguishing it from all other swords.

From this sword of the Word (Ephesians 6:17) come particularly a "peculiar people," meaning "one's very own" (1 Peter 2:9). The word *peculiar*, used in Titus 2:14, suggests "out of the ordinary." If there is one thing the leader did for the tube, it was that he made it out of the ordinary. It was lifted high into a new realm. You are His responsibility as you respond to Him.

Terry Atkinson

JUST AS CHRIST HAS TAKEN YOU

The shepherd took the river stalk. Christ has taken you, separated from where it was found and brought into a new relationship, so you "might know him," not now with river and mud but with Jesus Christ (Philippians 3:10). He will never dry up or flow low. He will never lack. He is never dependent on the rains. It was from rags to riches. What had been a muddy pool was altered into what is pure, clean, and usable. It, like Abraham, would be told to look to the hole it came from (Isaiah 51:1). It was no longer subject to the vagaries of changing water as the water swept by. It was a vessel fit for the master's use. Where once it had grown in the mud, surrounded by water, it would now cease growing in a plant sense, but now it would grow as music streamed from it—not now with flowing water but in a relationship with faithful fingers, as the master of sheep took hold of it.

New purposes were going to be driven through the reed as a plan not yet revealed. It went and was taken from one world into another, used in a different way. It might have been there originally to decorate the riverbank, but now it must become more than a decorative thing. It had to express the will of the leader of the sheep. taken into another realm, set apart for service, by His hand ordained. It was cared for by the sheep carer and set apart for use. They were the care and love of the sheep separator, for he knew the difference between a lamb and a goat. It seemed as if a newborn lamb had been placed into this common stalk. It would be more than a prized lamb.

IT GREW IN A DIFFERENT DIRECTION WITH A NEW PURPOSE

This reed, consisting of the nature grown with planted, grew in a different direction with a new purpose. Its existence before had been one of decoration, but now it was to become one of dedication, not now waving in the strong wind as a useless endeavor but used to help the shepherd in his spirituality.

From something as ordinary as decorating a riverbank, the friend of toad, water rat, and dragonfly would become part of its rescuer's nature, held in the hands of a man. His music stick had been part of the River Jordan, meaning "descender." In Adam's nature, it was downhill to hell. The reed would express his will. The wind had freely blown it in every and any direction. The rain had pelted it. Whatever it had come through, it would make it stronger for the purpose before it, in the hands of the one who cut it to set it free. Little did it know that in each raindrop there was the potential for music. In each snowdrop, there was music to be discovered.

In its history, as in yours, nothing was wasted. Every blow it felt, every pain, even the chafing and rubbing with the rolling in the hands of its rescuer, and everything it passed through. Every obstacle that forced it to go one way and another was put to good use in the future. It must pass through a process that would bring it into sanctification. The pipe dream wasn't a thing of chance but a prized possession with a new position in destiny. Here was destiny's child.

Even before one note sounded from the reed as part of a song, it meant it was the shepherd's. The bridge between the cutter and shaper was the music. We must sing to His tune. He had taken on onside and was sanctifying it through that one act, followed by many other deeds of helpfulness. We must let the truth be part of us, just as water had been part of this reed. Soak yourself in truth. Grow in truth, and if you do that, truth will set you and others free. There would be more than "water music" flowing through it. The moment it was lifted, it was separated. No matter where you took the reed, this didn't alter the fact that it was set apart for a better purpose to be used as it yielded in a better way. The mouth organ was set apart for service by God's hand ordained, the temple of the Spirit saved and sanctified.

THE REED PLACED WITHIN REACH

The reed was sometimes placed in the garment of the shepherd near his heart. On other occasions, it was put into his girdle, a reminder that in the book of Colossians love is like a girdle placed around the middle. In Colossians 3:14, that girdle is revealed as love that holds everything else together. The reed was put where it could hear the heartbeat of the sheep lover.

Sanctification has nothing to do with your geographical position. It has everything to do with a Christ- centered life, which makes you different from the world around you. Early Christian believers were thought of as being "eccentric," meaning "having another center." It was the apostle Paul who wrote, "For me to live is Christ, and to die is gain" (Philippians 1:21). Christians, no whatever happens to them, don't lose their shape or sense of calling.

Don't let any silly knock or unexpected blow send you out of tune. The rush doesn't change when it finds change. We need Christians to be as nails, so when they are struck with a hammer, they stick! They don't their shape, bend, or buckle under pressure. Through their sanctification, they hold on with rigor. This musical vehicle isn't like money that changed into many denominators. What is round remains round. What is square remains square. What has a sharp cutting edge, no matter how fierce the battle, keeps its cutting edge if taken to the Rock for sharpening, and then it is ultimately taken to the victory ribbon.

THE WORD OF GOD IS THE TRUTH

The Word of God (the truth, the whole truth, and nothing but the truth—the oath taken in an England court of law) becomes the throne of Jesus. You crown Him on that throne by your sanctification. The crown one wears, who is "all glorious within," is that of sanctification. It doesn't happen all at once. Like the reed, we couldn't understand the plan the Lord has for us. He gives little peeps of it now and again. We have the mentality and understanding of a sheep when it comes to the word *sanctification*. We don't understand that out of that one word, a plan appears. You are the "yes" of God in this world, His stamp, impression, and expression. The main difference for the reed pipe was in what the shepherd did "to" it and "for" it.

For the reed pipe to produce good music, there was no aimless slashing it with a spear or sword. It had to move from "reed" to "feed." It fed music to hungry spirits. It was the friend of those who needed it. It was like a promise from the Word of God. Its music used to get hold of people. It was the instrument that could stop men in their tracks and command obedience. You have listened to music played or to a good choir singing, and before you realized it, you were tapping out the tune with a toe. It slowly begins to take hold of your heart, and that is but the start.

The knife had to work incredibly careful on the reed. The redesigning of it was as careful as the stone sent from David's sling into the giant's head (1 Samuel 17:49–50). The giant never rejoiced or sang a song, but the nation of Israel did. Even a flying pebble or stone makes a particular sound in music. The reed, being cut, felt the hand that was drawing it closer to himself. There are certain pains to be born, as when a woman is in childbirth, when we are being brought into sanctification. There are in-depth plans in the pains. There are also crowns in thorns.

CHRIST'S LIFE ON DISPLAY IN YOU

Sanctification is defined as "Christ's life on display in you." You are God's shop window, His harvest. You are part of the travail of His soul. You are the advertisement for Christianity. You are the stained-glass window of the church. As a believer, you are a "saint," "one who lets the light shine through." Are you a good advertisement? Will your Christianity persuade any to come to Christ? Christian friend, you become the shop window. You are the mirror that reflects the nature of Christ. It is like having beautiful cream and peaches, caviar, and special spices on an old saucer. The Word of God (Old and New Testaments) is so important because it is through the Word that we are sanctified (John 17:17). Where it mentions being wholly sanctified (1 Thessalonians 5:23) it refers to our separation in our spirits from the spirit of the age we live in. It is the difference between chalk and cheese, water and wine. It is more than what we "do"; it is what are we "are" in Christ. I "am" what I "am" by the grace of God (1 Corinthians 15:10).

KNOWING WHERE YOU ARE AND WHAT YOU ARE

Sanctification is knowing "where" and "what" you are in God and letting it stream from you as a ray of sunshine on a cloudy day. God must work through you like music coming through a reed. Sanctify the Lord God in your heart (1 Peter 3:15), meaning, let Christ have a special place in your heart, and then the world will know that to you Christ is your treasure and the measure of the truth in you. Sanctification is a natural process once we have been cut and set free.

DON'T LET WHERE YOU ARE CHANGE WHAT YOU ARE

It was by the process of being cut and set free from muddy and swirling waters that the reed was sanctified. You can't be blessed into anything. Be like 1 Thessalonians 1:9, who "turned from idols to serve the living and true God." There was a purpose in the river stalk being cut and rescued. That which was rescued must go and through its music rescue others from doubt, fear, suicide, helplessness, and sorrow. Let this reed, your life, be the principal mourner at any funeral. Let it also be the chief guest at a wedding. Where it is won't alter what it is. Keep dipping a pebble or diamond into water, and it will neither change its value or shape. Change and decay are in all around we see, but it will remain the same because He who changes not abides with it. It just can't be an empty experience. Remember, the stick of music had come from swirling waters and lots of movement. Sanctification, setting you apart for His use, won't result in lack of activity, defined in a new expression of life and the nature of Christ seen through your everyday life. Being sanctified doesn't mean being dull or unhappy. It has no connection with being sad or looking religious. It is neither the cross you wear on your lapel nor the mobile telephone on which you carry your Bible.

THE EXPERIENCE OF BEING DEDICATED

Now the reed must enter the experience of being dedicated to the shepherd. It had already traveled far but not far enough. It was already yielded but not yielded enough. The pipe illustrates to us the heart of sanctification and dedication. One brought about the other, providing perfect balance for the reed. In His hands, we were tuned to truth. Our love sings the glory of God. It isn't what we say but what we let shine through us as luminaries in the dark world (Philippians 2:15). In this age, we are part of the age to come.

We have discovered in our Christian lives, as illustrated by the pastoral reed, that "consecration," the brother of "dedication," can mean "to fill the hands." Consecration is what you hold in your hands. It's what you have, not what holds or limits you. Dedication is what is in your heart. You are totally given to it, as a branch to the vine (John 15:5). That doesn't mean to fill the hands with anything, such as that representing wood, hay, sand, or stubble. It was "hot" sacrifice from the altar that was placed in the hands—held out as a token of surrender, since the priests were dedicated in Exodus 29:9, 24. There had to be the filling of the hand that flowed from the heart. The security of this reed stick was in the hands that were filled.

Your safety is in Christ. Position yourself in the hand, yes, the hand where the starting pistol is when any race is about to commence. It could never be done in meager measure. This doesn't mean we fill our time with good works, lined with fair speeches, and expect to ride triumphantly into heaven on the backs of those good works and fair speeches. We have been saved by faith. We are being saved by faith. We shall be saved by faith (John 3:17; 5:34; 10:9; Ephesians 2:8).

THE REED IS IN THE HANDS OF THE SHEPHERD

The reed is in the hands of the shepherd. When the priests were consecrated in Exodus 29:24, they held out their hands as a token of full surrender. These hands won't determine my destiny, but the sacrifice laid on them will be an illustration of my love for the Lord and my service to Him. To be dedicated, Jesus puts sacrifice into our hands little by little before we are trusted with the full heifer as it was about to be offered on the brazen altar (Numbers 5:25–26; 19:2, 5). There was nothing in that hand, so the Almighty could fill it. Their sacrifice was bloodstained and God reigned. They wanted to do something for God, but they wanted to do it with all their might. Here's my heart, and here's my hand, given as gifts to God. The "hand" represented the man. There was no man's fortune in his palm. The capital and future of each priest were in the hands of God. "Go and do the work I have placed in your hands"; that is dedication. Cold hands toward God need warming up with hot sacrifice. A sacrifice that is on fire will burn constantly. The sacrificed beast did it all. A piece of the sacrifice, whether sheep or cattle, was cut from the animal and placed in an outstretched hand.

THERE IS NO PLACE FOR EMPTY HANDS

In a measure, what was on the altar went into the hand of the outstretched priest. It might not have been set alight at that moment, but the eternal demanded that He had a hot sacrifice. This suggests sacrifice with passion. Sacrifice is never cold and calculating. You can't mathematically work it out on four fingers or a calculator. The surrender depicted, when the hand was outstretched, what this sacrifice would offer to others. What was received in one hand was passed on to others in the other hand. Jesus of Nazareth went about doing good (Acts 10:38). "Good" means doing it as it should be, doing it according to the standard of the Bible. What the priest received in his right hand he passed on with his left hand. Sacrifice is a two-handed thing. The flag knew this as the hand of the musician enfolded it.

Those gathered nearest to the altar felt the fire as it warmed them. The priests were living at that moment in a naked flame. The priests tasted sacrifice before receiving any from anyone else. They could smell it before they tasted it. The smoke, as it rose, filed their nostrils before anybody else breathed it in. They tasted and handled it; they knew what the message was that it contained. It was the means and message of another's death and offering.

The same hand to be laid on the head of the sacrifice for sin was the hand that stretched like a platform, built on with the sacrifice as the main element.

The pattern of the sacrifice found on the hand was covered in blood; where a plan could be sketched appeared in the life being offered. Before they ministered to anyone else, they felt the weight of that sacrifice in their hand. There is no place in the work of God for empty heads, hands, or feet that don't know where they are going or what they are doing. It belongs to the theological school, which says, "Then I cast it into the fire, and there came out this calf" (Exodus 32:24). Get something from the cross of Christ into your heart and hands, and whatever you do with hands, feet, eyes, or mouth, let it represent Him who died on the cross.

Terry Atkinson

LET YOUR LIFE EVER BE A MELODY

Consecration never means to light candles or wear garments that are ill fitting and uncomfortable. It isn't the constant repeating of the Lord's Prayer. Consecration never means or describes the experience when a bishop comes to lay hands on you. It comes from sour to a sweet reed with music sounding from it; this is your ministry.

Make me an instrument of worship. Make me a symphony of worship. Let my life ever be like a growing tree, every branch as truth that bears fruit in its season—ever telling of the Savor's truth. Another angle on the word *consecration* is to "fill-up" (Exodus 29:22). It is the act and piece that was missing between the people and the Lord. It completed their offering. The emptiness of the pipe was filled, not now with water but with music. It meant there was nothing stale about the music produced. Each morning a new song would sound among sheep. What had been static was now on the move, and it had a ministry into misery to move others.

It was as full of God as the cup that overflowed in Psalm 23:5, not just a full cup, since the hands of the dedicated priest were filled with sacrifice, but "full" and "running over." Sometimes what runs over, what appears through your life, is more important than what fills the cup.

The Great Shepherd brings to you all that was missing. Let me make the hills, chills, and ills of life be the backdrop for the music that comes from my life. If I follow the scales of truth, I shall produce that majestic music in my life, tuned to the truth, never out of tune, for if I am, it means I am out of touch and out of step with the Savior. For the saving Savior, be a singing saint in your dedication. Be as full as a flute is of music when played, for it is now used.

Eight

The Holiness of Believers in the Musical Reed

It wasn't long before the reed was severed from its old stock and way of doing things. Its days of dreaming in the sun or trying to hide from the storm were over and done with. It does take time, but it is God's time and timing when we are brought into "holiness," meaning "wholeness" and "oneness." Step by step, cut by cut, it was being transformed (2 Corinthians 3:18; 5:17).

As with us, after being brought from the old world of mud and swirling waters, the danger of being bent and broken, even taken and used for fire sticks, was something that wouldn't last the test of time but would go up in smoke. The hand that cut it would protect it in the future from the ravages of wild beasts and storms. The water reed was taken and held in such a grip as if the shepherd were holding a sheep to sheer it. In place of the old, everything would be new, as in "different." As there would be a flow of music through the flag, so let the life of Christ flow through you.

The Enrichment of Holiness

After this experience, as it was being arranged, it entered the enrichment of holiness. This is a quality defined as "rich" because it changes a beggar into a prince and a prince into a king as it turns a princess into a queen. It is holiness without which no man shall see God (Hebrews 12:14; 1 Thessalonians 3:13). "Holiness" is "healing." Holiness is having all torn or faded parts restored and put back together. He "restoreth" my soul. He "turns it back" (Psalm 23:3); that is holiness, when we who had our backs to the Lord are turned to face Him in the face of Jesus Christ. Instead of just following Him, we turn to face Him as we pray. The music stick always saw the face of the hill farmer as he played a tune on it. The look on that face is what we require to be reflected in our lives.

It is you being redesigned who has been predesignated (Ephesians 1:5, 11), you have had the old life rubbed out, and you are being redrawn. That isn't with graphite as in a pencil but through the rich, red blood of Jesus Christ. It is from the dead to dynamic. It is this experience that reveals the power of the shepherd, our Shepherd, for His hands are holy hands. The process of a pattern was beginning that would draw this water reed on onside, to make it into something higher and deeper. That ignoble would be transformed into that defined as noble. God has taken the foolish things of this world to confound the wise and the mighty of this world (1 Corinthians 1:27). The rose was beautiful compared to this reed. The grace of this story is that no music would every sound out from the Rose of Sharon. Its only beauty would be in its color and scent. What had been nothing was about to become the "son of Consolation," a Barnabas (Acts 4:36). That empty thing would reveal its true nature in the pattern of music that sounded through it.

This music was unique because it belonged to only one person. It was identified as his music, since the life we now live in the flesh belongs to only one person, and that is God. You can't go higher than God; that is why all you do, have, and are should be from above (Colossians 3:1). What came through the tube wasn't from its lips but from the lips of the one who owned it. In your holiness, speak "with" Him but speak "for" Him. Let God do the playing, and your part is to respond; that is your responsibility.

DEEP RELATIONSHIP PRODUCES HOLINESS

It wasn't the way it played music in the future that made it holy. It was its relationship with the shepherd that made it quite different from the thousands of grass reeds that lined the riverbanks—as swimmers, ready to take the plunge into these icy waters, but never able to do so. It wasn't how it looked, what it said, where it had been, or where it was going that brought this endearing quality into its life. The same knife that severed it would be the same knife that promoted holiness in its usefulness. It was lifted from plight to be made into a pattern. The thinking pattern of the pastor was etched into it. This reed was so different from anything else around it: sheep, hills, water, growth, forage, fruit, leaf, or branch.

Every experience it had would be that arrangement that would put it back together again in a different shape. It was in holiness shaped to share what it had and to be what it was arranged to be. There was no getting away from the fact, just like the blind man in John's Gospel (John 9:1–34), who was healed. It looked like him. His parents knew it was him. If you want to find out the holiness of people, talk to them, and they will soon dish up what they love. It was only when the water stalk was played that anybody knew the difference. It was a difference between mud and freshwater, grub and butterfly. This difference in life changes the character and conduct of the way we live. We have the purpose bred in us of being the servant of the Master. From the shavings and cutting acts of life, we are being made holy. Each life touched by the Good Shepherd declares "holiness unto the Lord."

CHANGED FROM ONE STAGE OF GLORY TO ANOTHER

It would be changed from one stage of glory to another (2 Corinthians 3:18). It would be holy because every part of it would be pieced together by the shepherd's hand. This musical instrument would have the artwork of the sheep gatherer implanted in it. It was the work of the leader in it that made it whole. It would mean that it was sacred to one thing, and in this instance that was music. It wasn't where it was kept or where it stood. It wasn't the place it was in that made it holy. It was what was put inside of it, described as leaven that "leavens the whole lump" (Galatians 5:9). People, hearing the music, sheep music, that came from it and the shepherd's music, would declare, "That is different." Here is a reed that makes music and makes you want to sing and dance. This is different from anything we have seen or heard before. "We never saw it on this fashion" (Mark 2:12).

Each Song Played Was a Sob

The hillside knew whose pipe this was through the music that sounded out from it. Each song was a sob from the sheep taker's heart. His tears were transformed into music. Notes from the bulrush trilled from it like tears falling from the eyes. As those tears cleansed the eye, so the music played cleansed and refreshed the spirit of the player. His tunes broke the silence and painted pictures on every dark cloud—sometimes quiet, other times soothing, sometimes played as if an army were marching through the glen. It was used as a poker in the fire to stir the spirit of all who heard it. Each note was a heartbeat of the shepherd, and it meant that this music stick was wholly given to the holder. The character of the stick became the character of the owner and player.

Some things are broken to stop others from using them. That is a true definition of consecration. You can now understand your pain. If we had no suffering in life, we wouldn't be half as useful and helpful. In our brokenness, we can experience holiness in wholeness, where, by the Spirit of God, we are made into that defined as holy.

The Japanese potter has a method of repairing a broken vessel, called *kintsuji*. It is a centuries-old method of repairing broken pottery. The sap is taken from a tree; then it is lacquered and dusted with gold, silver, or platinum. It is known as "golden joinery." Wherever the break has taken place, they line it with gold. That adds value to the object and makes a broken vessel of more value than just a normal clay pot.

Holiness was defined by the Greek and Hebrew language as that seen as an example of not changing when change it finds. To the Greeks, it was that way with the beauty of form. It was the sister of grace. It was seen in that defined as being different. This cut reed was so different from the other reeds growing along the bank of the river. Their destiny was in flood and water, rain, and strong wind, mud, and weakness as some were swept away. Their destiny was in the flowing river and where it might or might not take them. Holiness isn't the child of chance. This chosen reed was safe and as sound as it was holy, because it was given wholly to one thing. "This one thing I do" (Philippians 3:13). Its sacredness was found in the fact that it forgot its past and reached through its music into the future. It possessed a ministry in music that stretched beyond itself. It was never saved to serve itself. It was taken so that it might be taken, with what was brought to it, by the shepherd's kiss, since he used it to bring in the joker and mirth when sourness and disappointment were the order of the day. It could bring in the dawning of another day, whatever the hour was.

There Is a Cost in Being Holy

Sanctity can be seen in the person who takes their stand, whatever the cost; and while others may play in the mud, the holy ones run pearls through their fingers. Those who are "heavenly minded" are full of earthly good. As the melody sounded out across the plains, it always became a finger that pointed to the glory of the rainbow rather than the dark shadows of the moon or clouds of night. Your holiness can be like that of John Baptist, who proclaimed, "Behold

Terry Atkinson

the Lamb of God which taketh away the sins of the world" (John 1:29, 36). Nobody said, "What a great or good reed that reed of piety is." It was always the sunshine that came from the heart of the sheep director. When the sun in the valleys was obliterated by clouds and mist, then the reed became the sunshine for that period. You may not be able to shine like the sun or twinkle like a star, but you can be part of His holiness. I can't be the moon in its splendor, but I can be a moonbeam. You can let come out of you what God has put within. In the same way he directed the sheep, he directed the music from the reed. Here was the first musical director.

WHAT HAD BEEN USELESS WAS NOW USEFUL

Sometimes holiness is defined as that being even destroyed so that no other person will ever drink from a vessel (Joshua 6:19). The vessel had been designed for one thing and one person. It suggests that every door is slammed shut to common use. What had been empty was now full. What had been useless was now useful and fulfilling.

It was the stone and sling David used to fell the giant that became holy (1 Samuel 17:49). It became holy in that it was different. No other stone had accomplished what this stone achieved. The sword and spear, as the armor of the giant, became holy because they were put to another use, the use of glorifying the God of Israel. When this soldier king wanted to describe the sword of Goliath, he said, "There is none like that!; give it to me" (1 Samuel 21:9; 22:10), and that is how we should feel about holiness or any other doctrine that leads us closer to Christ.

THE PATTERN OF THE SHEPHERD'S HEART

Anything that forms a pattern from its surroundings and then is taken (and the pattern of the shepherd's heart is allowed to move through it) can be taken and used to declare, "Holy is the Lord" (Leviticus 11:44). Every sound that came from the tube told you there was something different about it. Reed tubes couldn't normally speak, but this one could; it could sing. If mountains could be moved by compassion, then this reed knew how, through its music, how to remove every obstacle that entered the mind of this lowly man of the hills. In its holiness it was his friend and confidant; it was his holy aid.

The root and branch with the fruit of holiness mean to "be different," as different as the Tabernacle was to other tents, as different as the pipe reed that had been blown in every direction by the winds and was always facing swirling waters. In comparison to that, being shaped from reed into a musical pipe was in the hands of the shepherd. It is through you being in His hands that you are made holy.

HOLINESS IS SEEING THE HAND OF GOD IN YOUR LIFE

When the Israelites looked for Moses in the cleft of the rock, all they saw was the hand of God covering him (Exodus 33:22). Holiness is seeing the hand of God working in your life. It is a revelation of the glory of God, the nature of Christ in you, that comes via the new birth (John 3:7). It is a display of the new nature, which is the nature of Jesus Christ (Colossians 1:27). Jesus was different, not in how He looked but in how He spoke. "Never man spoke like this man" (John 7:46). Holiness was sparkling in what He did, in how He lived, and in the miracles others saw Him perform. Seeing a wretch turned into a winner is part of devoutness. "Behold what manner of love the Father has bestowed upon us" (1 John 3:1). Since it means a "different sort of love," so holiness is a different style of life. Behold what manner of life is ours?

Holiness will make you stand out—not like a sore thumb but like something different, such as a pearl compared to a pebble. It will make you stand out just as the water turned into wine stood out (John 2:9– 10). There was no comparison between it and another. This sacredness is described in corn having all the chaff removed from it or in the process of that happening. It is the life of a different nature. It isn't something the flag had to put on or take off. It let its music do the walking, saying, and singing. It is that quality that makes you stand out as the general stands out among his troops. Holiness makes you stand out as a thoroughbred horse among nags. It means among ships you are Noah's ark. In holiness of life and conduct, you become the palace, when compared to the tenement building or the broken-down house in a row of houses. From shed and shack, you are becoming the latest design in construction.

HOLINESS IS TO BE DIFFERENT

Holiness means to be "unlike." It means to be as different from the world around you as the Bible is to any other book. It was part of the disciples because they had another center and were thought of as being eccentric. They perceived that they were "unlearned and ignorant men. They took knowledge of them, that they had been with Jesus" (Acts 4:13). Weeds and flowers, water and wine, sand and gold dust are unlike one another. You have been loosed from "being like" this age. Living the life of God is to be as different as the Sabbath day was to Israel; hence it is defined as holy. When God created the world in Genesis 1:1–10, it says that after He had created it, He saw that it was "good."

That is another definition of holiness. Holiness can never be a mixture of different sweets. It isn't "pick and mix." It can never be a piece of this and that. The Lord hates a dab and a dip of this and the other. If a form is a half man and beast, no one knows quite what it is. You can never run with the hare and the hounds if you want to be holy as God is holy (1 Peter 1:15). There is no patchwork quilt here. It must be all one in Christ. Where you "go" doesn't

Bruised but Not Broken

determine your holiness but what you "are." Its sacredness wasn't in where it could go but in where it would let the shepherd carry it. People might look at the shepherd and, if the pipe was sticking out of his clothes, see the pipe.

Holiness isn't a dead ritual. It can never be seen in a museum or static image. It isn't sameness but saintliness that must be seen to be believed. It wasn't seen in the reed stalk just being a reed. It was seen when the pipe was played and moved along the rows of sheep amid all the manure and dust, with bits of straw or hay blowing in the wind. It remained what it was. This wasn't blown by the wind; it was blown by its Creator, as He breathed notes of music into it.

HOLINESS ISN'T FOUND IN THE CLOTHES YOU WEAR

This experience isn't found in the clothes you wear or in how large a Bible you carry. The music stick looked like a reed; it didn't seem to be anything more. Wearing badges carries a little blessing. Holiness means you are different from this world, just as the ambulance is different from any other vehicle on the highway. It means being as different as the policeman is to the citizen. It will be this difference that is seen, heard, found, and known in the cut reed that produced music. That cutting edge gets into holiness.

Holiness is something we require, because we have been commanded to "be holy as God is holy" (1 Peter 1:15–16). God is different from all other gods. They have eyes but see not, ears but they hear not, feet but they can't walk or talk, love or lead. There is a definition of holiness as seen in the leaven taken from the flour (1 Corinthians 5:7). It is appreciated as a meal without anything that would ferment it. That means the addition of things that change its nature. It is a meal without leaven, which is a type of wickedness. The Christian life can never be "I set this paintbrush free, and this is what it painted!" There are the pattern and purity of holiness in any life lived for Christ. Live for Him as this musical stick lived for its master. A life that isn't left to chance, the vagaries of life or anything else, won't produce holiness. Holiness is something without a hole, defined as a rip or a tear in it. Nothing happened to the bruised reed that the shepherd's hand didn't sanction. The hand of the sheep keeper was written all over the pipe—"whose I am, and whom I serve" (Acts 27:23).

No matter which way you turned it, which place you took it to, or how deep you plunged it into the water, this didn't change the nature of its "wholeness" or "holiness." Holiness like love doesn't change when change it meets; it bears all things (1 Corinthians 13:7). Love never fails (1 Corinthians 13:5, 8). Throw it in the air, and it will land as it left the hand. That is true holiness. It isn't found in a shadow or a type but in a musical flute that is beyond equal. It is holiness that can and will turn water into wine when describing our old nature is changed.

MEN OF QUALITY WHO HAZARDED THEIR LIVES

The early believers were thought of as being holy. That is why the artist depicts them wearing halos. It meant there were "men of supreme quality who hazarded their lives." They hazarded their lives for Jesus Christ (Acts 15:26). The word *hazard* means "to throw the dice." It is a gambling term, suggesting those who are addicted. There is such a speech of holiness that comes from the believer's mouth, just as the choice of music from the reed came at the instigation and choice of its owner. Wherever the reed was found or lost, bruised or battered, it belonged to its creator and mover, just as you belong in your holiness to Jesus Christ.

EARLY BELIEVERS WEREN'T CLAY MIXED WITH IRON

There was nothing in them that created this awesomeness. They weren't chocolate soldiers that melted in the hot sunshine or wilted in the heat of the battle. These disciples, particularly Peter, were so awesome that some wanted his shadow, the one who had been a failure to pass over them as he walked by. They thought Christianity, not a soft option or a soft center. Their secret is revealed in the Acts of the Apostles. "That these men had been with Jesus" (Acts 4:13). They walked like Him; they talked like Him. You couldn't tell them apart. Holiness is to have Christ at the center, with everything else at the circumference of life. We have the holiness of the Bread of Life, which is given to others. The Bible is called the Holy Bible because it is different from any other book. It not only poses questions but also provides the answers.

If you triumph in holiness, you will triumph in everything else. Because the music pole was what it was intended to be, it was successful.

Nine

The Lost and Bruised Musical Reed

The day was darkening as it was ending. As the shutters of the day came down, it seemed to the hardworking shepherd as if they were closing in on his spirit. It seemed as if the day bowed down as if it had concluded its theater for the day. Twilight would be a fight with the night. The pasture man was like a boxer with no hands or arms facing a heavyweight champion.

As the day bowed out and introduced the night, the leader of the sheep suffered a hard day of chasing, saving, finding, seeking, carrying, caring for, and moving his sheep. He had the feeling we all sometimes have of wrecked ruin. He was so tired; it was as if he had climbed every mountain with twin lambs on his back. It seemed as if when he crossed the stream, carrying a sheep on his shoulder and two sheep, one under each arm as he crossed the river, that this was just a continuation as night fell. He fell with it.

THE SHEPHERD ILLUSTRATES WHAT CHRIST DOES FOR US

His work is an illustration of our Great Shepherd of the sheep and the work He does "for" us and "in" us. This caring for sheep bowed His head on a cross as the sins of the whole world were placed on His manly head (Matthew 27:45; Mark 15:33). Darkness descended on Him as a shroud. There was not only a crown of thorns there but also the cares of other people, who would come to know Him as Lord and Savior.

One consolation for this sheep manager was that he had his pipe of peace—you know, the conduit of dreams. In each note of music played, there was a dream that required fulfilling. When he played sweet music through it, it soothed his spirit, calmed his fevered brow, and brought the shattered pieces of his heart back into place. As he played on his tube after heavy rain or a storm, a rainbow always filled the night sky. The first star to shine during the dawn period was the song from the water reed.

He felt it was time for the tube of tunes to make an appearance and an announcement. That announcement would be "Everything in the night sky is shining bright, and God is in His heaven." It could become a trumpet sounding the victory over the coming night. To the man of the hills, the reed wouldn't be as the cock that crowed when Peter denied his Lord (Matthew 26:34,74–75). There would be no "petering out" here.

He warmed his hands over the small fire and reached into his garments, aiming for his heart, to take hold of his prized possession. He couldn't believe it! There was no pastoral pipe. Something or someone had somehow snatched his pipe of praise from him. He had been robbed without realizing it. Had some armed robber come clandestinely in the dark and seized his treasure from him? Songs for the night had been stolen from him. What should he do? Tears began to cloud his vision, and sheep appeared as if they might be wild animals as his eyes misted over.

The fire suddenly began to go to ashes. It seemed as if the night sky had fallen. Here was a calamity worse and more in-depth than Job had experienced. This was like losing his best friend; this *was* his best friend. It was his nightcap, his medicine. The place where he had kept the musical box was empty, but more profound and hurtful than that, there was a place in his heart that was hollow.

Terry Atkinson

We All Have Bad Nights and Bad Dreams

Was there ever an endless night as long, deep, wide, or dismal as this one? This was the night of the long swords stabbing into the heart of the shepherd. He felt more robbed than the time of the stealing of his sheep. A bear would have been happier when deprived of its whelps. This night was a night of bad dreams and terrible nightmares. Here in the ashes of the fire, it wasn't a phoenix that rose to live again. It was hopelessness, depression, like a dragon appeared that required killing. How could he now kill what he felt because his armor had fallen from him? He had stood before with the reed pipe as two, and now he felt like one as if he had been cut in half. He was like a man with two good eyes, who suddenly became blind and would have to grope and grasp his way through day and night. What had been a rose garden was suddenly turned into a wilderness of wild thought.

If the flute had been a sheep that had gone astray, its bleating would have been its discovery. The leader of the sheep would have gladly scoured hill and vale looking for it. If it had been a knife, staff, or rod, even a coin that had been lost, he could have searched for it. The lost couldn't be found because he couldn't remember where it had been lost.

It is so tricky when searching in your memory; you find it isn't the Aladdin's cave you thought it was. What it was, where it had been were lodged in his memory, but the facts of departure were missing. The pastoral brush had taken up its stand and allowed for nothing else to take its place, but some an enemy had dethroned and denied its existence. It was irreplaceable, even irreparable, since it had been irrepressible when music played, making the guider of lambs a one-man band. He couldn't go back to the beginning, for there was no beginning or ending.

SOME THINGS CAN NEVER BE REPLACED

There wasn't a sound except silent mockery as the shepherd wiped his brow. The only noise to replace the music was the mocking crackle of the twigs as they now burned because he had fed the fire. What would feed his tormented spirit in the night? The flames from the fire were laughing and dancing, but he wasn't. The darkness in his mind began to deepen as dawn began to break. He thought, *Well, at least I have the "breaking" of the light to comfort me.* Tears again filled his eyes as if molten lead were being poured into a mould. It was the word *breaking* that had turned dry eyes into wet patches. Here was a battle raging in his emotions. He would never win this losing battle, because his chief armor bearer was missing. It had gone AWOL (absent without leave).

After struggling for so long, dawn began to appear. If only the reed tube could sing like the dawn chorus again. Wasn't it Job who had cursed the day of his birth (Job 3:3, 16)? Who was it who said, "All these things are against me" (Genesis 42:36)? Wasn't it another who had to be a day and night in the deep (2 Corinthians 11:25)? In modern language, these thoughts galloped through the seeking, loving shepherd's mind. He should give up on the thing. This thought argued in his mind. It shouted in his mind, "Not this lost reed but give us another one." He experienced a tug-of-war. After all, the easiest thing would be to cut another reed from the riverbank or stream. A new one would produce original tunes. There would be the delight in his hands due to his artistry in carpentry. These thoughts became hurdles he must jump.

How should he look for it if he wanted to look for it at all? Maybe it had gone down the river it had been taken from? It wouldn't stand out in the darkness, and that was why he must wait for the sunshine of the day to help him find his long-lost friend. He gathered his things together as he gathered his thoughts, trying to get his ideas to obey him rather than to command him.

Terry Atkinson

Rediscover the Map for Your Life

Jesus Christ never gave up on you. "I will never leave thee nor forsake thee" (Hebrews 13:5). When you fell or was lost, He came to where you were and called you in your state to Himself. Wanderer, wonder no more, for the man with the map of life has come to where you are. He doesn't demand that you play His music. He comes to you, lifts you, and commences playing the tune of the "Delights of Being Found." No one ever searched for you like this Shepherd. He didn't just go through a valley or over the hill and far away. Jesus traveled from heaven, looking for the reed Adam had lost when he transgressed in the garden of Eden (Genesis 3:9–11). As that garden began to produce weeds, so the loss of the pipe began to sow seeds of doubt and despair in his mind; both joy and peace were murdered (Genesis 3:18). These torments didn't come in ones but as a whole pack of wolves to ravage his spirit.

Not only was the river flag lost and under attack from an unseen enemy, which had entered his mind as the day ended. Suicidal thoughts began to pierce his soul. He felt fragmented as something broken that could never be pieced together. The former pattern of things had been ripped apart. The dove of peace that had flown into the heart of the green pasture and quiet waters with an olive branch in its beak had been shot as it flew from his heart as a form of escape and disappeared into the ashes of the fire (Genesis 8:12). Cupid with the arrows started missing the target.

Sometimes Going Back Means Going Forward

Just at that moment, he looked again and again; like a watchman at the city gates, he peered with such a gaze as would have taken him into eternity. He turned to go back the way he had come. After all this, he would have fond memories of his flute. The memories of the musical, moving moments walked and talked with him as if he were being accompanied by a friend, who was bringing consolation to his heart. The seeker's feet trod as if lead had been poured into his feet.

His memories and achievement, born through the music played on the tube, were still with him. His walk was that of one attending a funeral, his own. With his head bowed, face expressionless, his feet shuffled along the dusty road. He was like a child being sent to a school they didn't want to attend. It was as if his heart were rejecting the songs as he went along. Maybe he could sing the thing back into usefulness.

He had traveled many miles, draped in a black gown of sorrow, stitched with remorse. The man of the vale was looking for signs as to where his lost reed might be found. It was then, as he came around the bend and peered into the stale footprints of the sheep that he saw the pipe reed. It was partly buried in the prints of the sheep, and to add to its insult, a piece of sheep's dung nearly covered it. It looked like something wearing a mud pack! That moment was like the signature of a thousand-pound banknote! It was half buried—hurt, dirty, crushed (not unwanted), and unknown—but not unsought or unloved.

It was with glee that the excellent shepherd embraced it, with the same hug of the prodigal son's father as he fell on his neck (Luke 15:20). His winner had come home! The footprints of the seeker had become the footprints of the finder.

CHRIST AS THE SHEPHERD REACHES US

The love in the heart of the sheep carer burst its banks as he reached forth to take it to himself to examine it. He wanted to catch it and touch it with deep love. There was the desire to grab it and scold it for getting lost. Then he had to remind himself that this was an inanimate object. He blamed himself for its loss or, should he say, its being laid aside for a moment, if only to test his deep love for it. Reaching for it was like getting and taking hold of his favorite piece of fruit or taking hold of a long-lost sheep. He would have kissed it before he washed it, but there was no desire to add dung and dirt to his breakfast.

The journey had been so long, but finding what he had been seeking was worth it all. Finding it made all the hard struggle and long night worth it. In finding it, it seemed as if the tube was already playing music in his heart. Jesus Christ thought you were worth the long journey from heaven to earth.

WE CAN ALL START AGAIN

The shepherd's eureka moment had come! He had found his heart's desire in this lost lyre. His joy knew no bounds. What he felt could never be manacled hand and foot! If only it could be bottled and sold to other shepherds. Here, in essence, was the apostle Paul and Silas, singing in prison at midnight (Acts 16:25). The beauty and fragrance of it all were that he could start afresh with the tube as if nothing had ever happened. Would he be able to play the same tunes? Had this mishap—or should he call it a calamity—be the shortening of the musical reed? Had its loss robbed him of hidden musical ability? Could he trust himself with it ever again? These thoughts and many others seemed to grow as blades of grass, the grass of tender pastures that surrounded him.

The reed looked wrecked and forlorn. It appeared on the ground like nobody's child. Can a bombed bridge be walked over again? Can what is broken and blighted be used and trusted in the future? Even trusted with his future? If it had been a drawing in the soil, he could have rubbed it out and started again, hoping that the second time of trying would be the best. The best was yet to come.

You Can Become So Many Things in His Hands

In the seeker's hands, it could become a harp, a cornet, a dulcimer, an all-singing, dancing tube of tunes. It was the valley conqueror who would decide this. The decision wasn't as easy as determining which sheep would become pregnant and bear twins in the spring. All the musical reed had experienced we experienced when Christ found us. It had fallen, it had slipped, and it had lost its position (Ephesians 2:1). While lost and hidden, it was no longer near the heart or in the hand. It was covered in some foreign matter. It was tuneless. It was stuck in the mud. It was going nowhere. The musical child of the man of the sheep had become somebody else's child. He could adopt it. His love child had become a renegade—not through its own fault but because of the carelessness of another. A slip had become a trip, and a trip had become a fall.

No matter how bright the moon shone or how clear the pathway was lit before it, the reed had been stuck in a hole. It couldn't get out of its own volition. It's music meant nothing because a distance had appeared between itself and the one who would make it talk music.

How descriptive this is of us being away from the Lord of all glory. The true story of our reconciliation is found in these words. The reed was lifted, it was loved, it was cared for. It was turned over gently. It was lovingly turned over and over, even washed in the finder's tears. Here were the action and reaction of love. He made a vow under his breath, never to lose it again. Maybe he should tie it around his middle with a cord of love.

Let the Lord Decide Your Future

The pipe of dreams was brought into another realm. It was another hand that determined its future, not its own. It had experienced being lifted, loved, and translated from one kingdom into another (Colossians 1:13). What had seemed Greek to others now was fully understood as it heard the good man's voice. It meant that its dreams had been resurrected. It could live on again in the power of resurrection life.

It was in a place called Ruin Ravine that it was found. The shepherd knew it well. He had fallen there only the previous day and badly bruised himself. So he understood the bruises the music flag suffered. He was acquainted with them in its sorrows and despair. The ravine was scattered with mutton bones. Local shepherds and sheep knew it well. Many a lamb had entered in like a lamb and had come out of it as lamb chops. This place was a chopping block for sheep.

The hand that had lifted it from the ravine was bloodstained and marked with thorns, indicating that the shepherd had suffered when he first fell; and then found the reed, but here was unmeasured grace. It was sought for again. Jesus Christ, as this sheep leader, seeks again and again, high and low, near and far for us (Luke 15:4). The steps of the seeking heart led to where it was amazing grace. At the reed's darkest moment, the sun shone in meridian splendor, as seen in the face of the shepherd. If the bruised reed had been human, the first thing it would have seen would have been a smiling face—the face of its rescuer, lover, friend, and musician. The hand that lifted it would keep is close and free forever. That hand became an anchorage for something that had been through a storm. If alone, it could have played "three cheers"; it would have done so as it was found and lifted from a specific grave and from an uncertain future into something as substantial as a copper bottom.

Jesus Christ Makes You Worth Everything

It was the sheep leader and keeper who made it worth something of everything. Money couldn't pay the price to have it found and lifted. It took love, deep and long, suffering and seeking love. What had been limited was lifted into an unlimited experience. Through this music machine, love, joy, mercy, kindness, and grace sounded out. The trees of the fields would clap their hands (Isaiah 55:12). It is Jesus Christ, the good, great, and glorious Shepherd who gives value to any life and to everything that is surrendered to God. This ignoble reed became noble by a searching, caring shepherd, who would make it of more value than a pigskin pursed. It would be valued above every silver shekel that would be in any purse. The debt had been paid that it couldn't pay by One who had paid something He didn't owe.

May you surrender to Him. It is through association that some things are valued. If you obtained the crown of Henry VIII, the fact that it was a crown would make it valuable, but because it belonged to a monarch, it was made more useful. If you were the owner of William Shakespeare's pen, then it would be of such great value— not because you owned it but because of its history. While lost, that history would have been a mystery, but because of it being found and converted, that history would become His story. It is Christ who makes the believer into a rare measure of a treasure, called "my peculiar treasure" (Psalm 135:4). The Great Shepherd only adds value and virtue to us. Can you put a price on being rescued and having eternal life?

The finder would become the keeper. The reed was taken with a firmer grasp than mud could ever give, and it was examined under the gaze of love from above. The pleasure of the face was the measure of it being found. A prodigal had returned to the fold (Luke 15:5, 24). The wandering sheep had been followed and brought back into the fold of music. This was a time of great rejoicing as the rays of a new day and beginning fell on the reed tube of rescued music.

Ten

The Bruised Reed Raised from the Dead

When the pipe reed was lost, it seemed to be dead, forgotten, and buried, but that is only part of the glory of this story. It was laid aside only for a while, just as we are at death (1 Thessalonians 4:16–17). No one saw a future for it, except the man of the sheep. It had to be buried, covered, and out of sight for it to be found and resurrected. Whether it had been buried deep or placed in a shallow grave of mud and sheep droppings, it would and did receive the same treatment.

The reed illustrates that when we die, there is life after burial (John 14:19). For anyone who has never seen an acorn grow into an oak tree, it would seem like an impossibility. There is a life after the planting in the deep earth. See any tree in winter—bare, barren, and looking lifeless—and spring seems impossible. Any seed or bulb placed into the ground dies; then it is resurrected, whether as a rose, tulip, or Solomon's tears.

The bruised reed was resurrected when the shepherd came and lifted it from its unknown grave. There was no epitaph where it fell; there was no evidence of where it was. It had no voice to call for help. It lay there like a helpless object, robbed of its life and youth. Its days of musical treats were over and done.

When it fell into the soil, it went from a position of strength to weakness.

It could have fallen into the grave of the unknown.

When any musical instrument is on onside, nobody cares; nobody seems to take any notice until it is required. Even the scriptures say that where a tree falls, there shall it be (Ecclesiastes 11:3). The first thing that happens when a reed is retaken is that it is retuned; it is made fit for the purpose chosen. Sought for because of the man who led animals, it was necessary. It was his creation lost or found, appearing, or disappearing. There would have never been any flowers placed on this grave, because nobody knew where it was. The power and purpose of its resurrection were in the hand of the shepherd, as ours will be in the capable hands of the Chief Shepherd, Jesus Christ (1 Peter 5:4).

We Will All Rise from the Dead

The body of the bruised reed had work done to it to turn it into something special. It was reformed and made into a more capable instrument, achieving what it would never have accomplished in its old body. At the resurrection of the dead, we shall be as this pipe was (1 Thessalonians 4:17; 1 Corinthians 15:51–52). We shall be shifted and raised to see the face of our Seeker, who found us, for they "shall see His face" (Revelation 22:4). We who have gone out of tune at death—some with broken strings, others totally out of tune with this life on earth—will be restrung and retuned. Most seem to be crushed and bruised by death. Your new body will arise as the music of another sphere, an instrument in the singing of the song of Moses and the Lamb (Revelation 15:3). Every song, as every voice, will be perfect then. There will be no instrument string a wrong note. Nothing will be off-key or out of sorts.

The water stalk would arrive through a power outside of itself. It was an upward life that would result in the body of the tube changed. This resurrection into a new life of new dimensions wasn't dependent on the reed without music. It had fallen to the level of the sheep's hooves. It had made its bed in the mud until one came to wake it from the dead.

Was it the shepherd's reed that lay at his feet? It looked like a reed, but it was so bruised and caked in mud that it wasn't easy to recognize in the dawn of the day. Could this cold and still flute ever play music again? Would it ever be played to skipping lambs? Had the rub of the hoof and the snare of the soil spoiled it forever? Its cold, forlorn shape offered no evidence of what was about to happen. The finder, who was keeper, had some new plans for it.

Did he pass through here as he led the sheep? Was this strangled and stranded pipe something that belonged to another shepherd? Suddenly, the keeper of sheep's mind became a tunnel with many trains of thought passing through it. He recognized it through the scoring marks he had made on its body. These marks marked it out as belonging to him. It wasn't the prize or possession of another, and it was his tube of tunes. There lay the musical pipe without music, without a song, without even a whistle or chirp, pierced and bruised by a fall.

LET CHRIST DEAL WITH YOUR SUFFERINGS

Buried, battered, christened in the rain, forlorn, it was taken up into another realm as we shall be at the rapture (1 Thessalonians 4:17). It looked like a tunnel underground that had caved in on it, so disfigured that it was difficult to distinguish it from other debris lying around. The sheep shearer's marks were in it. It had his seal in its body. Nobly could make the marks that his knife had made in the music tube, identified because it had suffered for a while, brought in from the cold. It was lifted to a new realm, where it was restored—lifted "out" to be taken "in" into the warmth of His bosom. It was Jesus who said, "That where I am, there ye may be shall also" (John 14:3).

It was in hell without the flames. Buried in the unknown grave of a fallen hero, this fallen hero required rescuing and loving, washing and healing—just as we need these things when coming to Christ. It was walked all over, trodden underfoot. It was hopeless, left bleeding and dying on the Jericho Road (Luke 10:30). If the guide of sheep took the tube back to himself and used it, it would mean that he had created this object of music twice—once when he first cut it free from its old nature and now a second time as it was lifted in love to be rescued and used. It was given a second chance to reveal the majesty of music.

This happening, my friend, is the gospel story of how the old reed, Adam, fell by transgression. It is the story of being found and formed twice. God created humankind. Adam fell in the garden of Eden but was rescued back to God via the garden of Gethsemane.

All were rescued twice. God created us in the beginning, but then He recreated us in Christ Jesus, formed twice—found and formed when the gospel informs us of Christ.

THERE IS GREAT POTENTIAL WHEN THOSE LOST ARE FOUND

While a gold coin is lost and buried, it is worthless and useless, but once discovered, it has a power all its own. Once fallen, it hides what it is. The sovereign's head is covered in dirt. The power that always resided in it is freed once it is found and put back into circulation.

There were a thousand images in his mind of the lost tube. None of them seemed to fit the description of what lay in his hands. What had been battered could be bettered. That lost was now found. The sheepman could feel the music already formulating in his mind as he took what was called his "tuning knife." That knife, or the Word of God, had a thousand hidden beauties in it.

The early-morning mist was giving way to meridian splendor of the sun, seeing a thing found and rescued. The moment was his hour of rejoicing. Is was his moment of sheer joy, not superficial joy, which came through thinking of eating food or fruit, but the deep-down joy that takes pleasure without measure. What happened was his moment of the Appian Way experience, as Romans soldiers marched up it with their spoils of war. The City of Reed had been found and taken. Music, music, and more music would now be his.

The water he drank from the stream at his feet would taste like wine spiced with joy, the joy of the wanderer returning. Music without measure, creating exquisite, crowned pleasure.

It would never if left to this arranger and finder find itself looking like a worm or slug in the soil. The hand that lifted it would be its crowning glory. The flute belonged to a higher realm. There could never be a throne of music in mud; it would require the dexterity of the herdsman's hand, knife, and lips. It would ascend as the skylark and be part of an anthem. There would be no empty wind blowing through it. What seemed to be a discarded object was found, and because it was found, it was made valuable. This musical rod would yet remove sorrowful tears, limiting those tears to what they should be and restricting them from becoming a flood the shepherd could drown in along with his sheep. It would fill every hole and level every mountain standing in the way of the will of the leader performed. Every dark and dismal hole would be filled with the light of music.

God Has New Plans for Your Life

From the valley where it was lifted, the keeper took the reed to clean it and see it reinstated next to his heart. It was a sudden thing, a rapture—not a rapture into chaos but into what is highly organized with a trumpet sound. After being found, it would now be baptized, signifying another death.

It was carried out carve by carve, step by step, puncture by puncture until it appeared as a new tube with a new song but in the hands of an old master. Suddenly, the keeper of sheep's mind became a river with many fish swimming in it. There lay the musical pipe without a tune, without a song, without even a whistle or chirp, pierced and bruised by a fall, even as it lay in his hand as some dead thing. He had new plans for it. The sounds that never came from the beak of a singing bird would come through this tunnel of love.

The man of the mountains would convert every discordant sound into a sound of the music of the hills and make them live. The reed was buried, battered, and covered with lost memories. He could crush it, throw it away, and start again. Through seeking it, as the moments dragged along, as his feet dragged through mud and mire, the love of this man of the fold was widened, deepened until it became immeasurable. The pastoral reed looked like a thrown-down altar. It had been so alone, but now, counting the sheep, it would be taken to an innumerable company, which on man could number as all the flocks gathered and were watered. It would reign in life again (Romans 5:17). This fallen hero was about to be rewarded with a new long-lasting life in the presence of the shepherd, just as we are in His presence (2 Corinthians 5:6, 8). It would seem as if the least musical instrument in the orchestra was promoted from second fiddle to the lead instrument. It had required rescuing and loving, washing, and healing, just as you required these things when Christ sought and found you.

We Are Lifted in Love to Love Others

What was it that made the sheepman seek, stop, and stoop to save the bruised reed? Reeds were as plentiful as sheep, nearly as plentiful as stones in the valley. The sheep were the material riches of the guide. In this reed was the majesty of music, which no lamb could ever bring to the soul of the shepherd. To save it, the shearer of sheep had to come down to the level of the fallen pastoral reed. Bending down on his knees, he lifted it as he loved it. He wanted to treat it as if it had never fallen. He wanted it to represent a medal given to him for bravery—the bravery he had showed when seeking to find it.

There is great joy in finding what is bought, sought, and surrendered. When he found it, it was a musical wreck-a boat without water. It was a reed coracle grounded up the creek without a paddle.

You Will Not Be Downtrodden Forever

What was it about this "ground organ" he loved? In another life and other circumstances, it might have been a "grand organ." Even though it had fallen lower down, it contained no music in the lower or minor key, no music of any kind without the help of the man.

Let me remind you that when Jesus Christ found us, there was no merit in us (Romans 7:18). Made from mud and sinking, some quicker than others, we weren't sinking in "quicksand"; we *were* the "quicksand." The flute reed, coming from the heart of the lover of beasts, was sought by the same shepherd.

When found, it felt an upward tug, more substantial than the downward spiral. It had the marks of being "downtrodden"; hence, where he found it, it was at the bottom and not at the top. The beggar on the dunghill had suddenly become a prince (1 Samuel 2:8). It went from mud to majesty, from death to life, from being lost to being found by a firm friend.

When things surround you and you feel you are sinking, and there is no deeper depth for you to sink to, look for and find a loving hand that has come to your rescue. It is the hand of help, the hand of the handyman, the hand of a faithful musician, who orchestrates the worlds with one word of his power (Colossians 1:16). He wants to stir slumbering cords and move across your heart again until your life becomes a symphony of worship, a symphony of sympathy for others who have fallen.

Reconciliation Is a Wonderful Thing

This reed would become rarer than any other reed. It was a tube of distinction because what was lost had been found. The shepherd sighed with relief that he had found his musical friend again. The sighting of it would remove it from moaning, then into singing. The reed would rule the valleys again. What sights into a song, a song that would blight every morose mood and feeling of failure in the guider of the sheep's heart?

They were together again, never to part—no repairing in the repair shop. The sheepman was the repairer of the breaches that had badly bruised it. The stalk discovered that love could cover so many hurts and misunderstandings. The heart of the finder and defender would become its keeper, and the keeper would become its tuner; it would be tuned into the finer feelings of pastoral life.

Jesus Christ Will Come Again

The shepherd now appeared a second time, coming to the aid of the bruised reed and reminding us of the Second Coming of the Great Shepherd of the sheep, Jesus Christ, who will come a second time to us in our experience of bruising (John 14:3). We, too, are going to experience the Second Coming of that Great Shepherd of the sheep (1 Peter 5:4). When Jesus comes, ah, that will be the day when the day breaks and shadows flee away (Solomon Song 2:17). What the man of the meadows accomplished in our text (Matthew 12:20) changes everything, and so will Jesus Christ when He returns.

Terry Atkinson

Your Body Is Going to Be Changed

Taking this old, crushed body of ours, He will redesign it. From the mud and muddle of this life, a new man or woman will appear. We leave this life with doors and windows wide. This body of humiliation will become a body of glory (1 Corinthians 15:47–52). The old body reformed into something that will last forever (1 Corinthians 15:35, 38–39). This life has known change and decay, but we are going into something that will last forever. As the carer of sheep had the hope within him of finding his flute, so we have this hope within as of Christ coming again (John 14:3) and resurrecting us into something better than music, which can lose it appeal, or music that can be off-key. When He arrives, everything will be re-tuned to the tune God is singing. They shall sing a new song. We await the dawning of a new day (2 Peter 1:19).

That mud surrounding the bruised reed was removed and wiped away. The grave will open, like a door no man can shut. In the coming resurrection, reeds will be turned into flowers. The tree stump will scent water again and flower. The stamping feet of the sheep will be removed. The awful smell of sheep dung will be replaced. Sweet-smelling perfume will fill the air. The feeling of being wet and forsaken will be taken away. Loneliness will be gone, crucified forever. Isolation will be but a memory as we enter the number no man could number (Revelation 7:9).

The surroundings of the reed were changed as it was lifted and carried away (1 Thessalonians 4:17). What has been long forgotten and cast on one side will be taken and used just as the shepherd did with this pastoral reed. Keep looking, waiting for His coming the second time and without sin unto salvation (Hebrews 9:28).

WE SHALL BE RAISED INTO HIS PRESENCE

The flute, raised by the hand of the shepherd, was raised into His presence, completed. The music reed, once dead and buried, had lost its music. There was the parting of music and reed. The music was left in the hands and breath of the sheep leader.

When you die, you leave that real you, your character, your new man, in Christ—with your Shepherd, Jesus Christ. We are more than just a feeble flute, more than just a body, made of different parts, separated at death. Your body goes to the grave. Your spirit is left with your Creator, just as the music was left with the sheep carer. The grave or cemetery described in the Greek language was an inn where travelers spent the night after they traveled from one destination to another. (See author's book *Dying Is Living*.)

EVERYTHING REUNITED IN THE RESURRECTION

The two, your body and character, will be brought together again at the resurrection from the dead. Without music, the reed was just a hollow tube. The music, the ability to soothe, smooth, and cheer, came from the two united. Untied, they were both in different areas. The body isn't important, although while in this life we place great importance on it. We don't believe in soul sleep. We believe that "absent from the body is present with the Lord" (2 Corinthians 5:6–9), suggesting "getting home." When Christ returns just as the shepherd returned, music and tube brought together again, we are going to be reunited and united when raised from the dead. The box, the body, will find its perfect peace when the hands and breath of the Shepherd restore it. It will be the dawning of a new day when all the shadows of the night have died. There will be no more night (Revelation 21:25).

Eleven
The Bruised Reed's Reflections

There was no music in the mud, no light in the darkness, no laugher in pain. There was only the music of the "ouch" bruised like you (Psalm 40:1). It was your experience while being in difficult circumstances. "I waited patiently for the Lord; and he inclined unto me and heard my cry." In waiting, I waited, I waited, I waited. The Hebrew tense of "waited" means waiting in darkness because one is robbed of potential. There were those in the New Testament who sat in the darkness and saw great light (Matthew 4:16). There is an influence of Christ Jesus in your life. He appears as a door of light, opened to reveal to you the way through and out.

The telling of the story of the bruised reed is like reading a page or pages of our diaries. Day after day God seeks for the unbeliever, sought in grace, by grace, and through grace (Isaiah 10:4). It is the grace that says, "I forgive you; now you forgive yourself." Mud, slime, river, other lashings, and any unmeasurable force gale quieted your heart. You have experienced a spiritual heart transplant. That storm, measuring "force ten"—the Ten Commandments—was converted into "force one," the love of God, the first and last commandment (Matthew 22:38–40). This unmerited favor (grace) drew a line where to stop or build a fence to keep Christ out, but it opened a door, even taking it off the hinges and allowing you. It drew you into the heart of grace, as if this flag were lifted by the hand placed around it. That was the beginning of the sheltering of the reed flute. These things became part of the memory of the reed. Peter reminded us in his epistle to "stir up your mind by way of remembrance" (2 Peter 1:13; 3:1). The sign in your life says, "No fishing here." In the open sea, it was removed, since everything would have been a barrier to the rescuer when rescuing the reed. The best way for Jehovah to help you is if you remove all obstacles to free grace.

THE TEARS IN THE SOB OF THE SHEPHERD

There were the sobs of the Shepherd as he found you, as the wanderer, mingled with delight. Whatever the lamb leader felt about this golden reed, looking back, Jesus felt about you. Jesus did more than cry over you; He shed great drops of blood, sweat that was turned to blood because of His depth of suffering (Luke 22:44). Those sobs and effort contained the tears that baptized you. They were those tears that quickened your emotions and taught you to forgive and forget.

You never required a round crystal ball to read your future from, because your future was in His tears and sweat drops of blood. Your future rescue isn't in the stars but in the Bright and Morning Star (2 Peter 1:19). Now you don't need to accept the horror of a horoscope reading, which has no scope of truth in it, for it is just false guesswork, giving an incorrect guess word. The plan for your life didn't require you to work it out, because the man of the meadows poured it in, pressed down, shaken together, and running over (Luke 6:38). The open seven seas held no Treasure Island for you, because just as the reed was found in the shepherd, you have been seen in God.

The music box was lost, brought to an open place. There were no long grasses where you were brought to; everything was naked and open unto the eyes of him with whom we have to do (Hebrews 4:13). There were no holes in your security system, where some beast might spring out and crush you, thinking that the cracking of your slim bones was music, the music of the diner when His hand claimed and covered your life.

The tears in the sob of the shepherd, when he found you, were one of those tears Jesus shed through unbelief as He raised Lazarus from the dead (John 11:33–36). It was a tear from this sob that softened sinners, dried a clay heart, and turned it into something malleable, soft, and tender. It was part of those tears of Jesus that went into the bowl from which He washed His disciples' feet (John 13:12). The tear was expanded until it became an ocean of love without measurable depth. You need to have this thing scribe over your heart. Fond memories are flowers that will never fade, and they are perennials. You, as the bruised reed, required these tears to be turned into an ocean. Your horizons and borders would enlarge or be removed. The Lord wanted to take you and has taken you to such depths and into such expanses that you can't see the coastline. If you wanted to return to the beggarly elements of this world, you wouldn't know where to start or finish.

The reed was found, inspected, and changed; there wasn't just one thing the shepherd's knife accomplished in it. The first cut was the prince of many that would follow. Your ladder of success and acclaim was the finger on the hand of Christ. There was a succession of activities that brought about assurances, which would be of eternal consequences. Looking back can sometimes take you forward. When dry and thirsty begin, think and thank the Lord for what He has done in your life. Don't be just another bleating sheep. Be something different. Let each memory be a squeezed grape.

Being lost, you had no future. Esau sought God without repentance, and although he wept, he didn't find what he was seeking, because he required more than his tears (Hebrews 12:16–17).

Bruised Reed, You Have Been Restored

Your testimony is that you were not only the gate locked and barred, but you were unhinged. You weren't just one with a slate loose, but you were bombed. Being found, believer, you felt it was like the petals of the rose opening to sunshine. Any aspirations you had, as the bruised reed in the hands of its keeper, would soon be restored. "He restoreth my soul" (Psalm 23:3). In the word *restore*, we collect the thought of being "rejuvenated." It means to be "brought back." It suggests in the word *restoration* the restoration of a fading picture.

It means to be turned back like a wheel that has come off the axle of the cart. It means to be turned around in the place that is yours so the real you may appear as a newly constructed wagon wheel, which depends on the axle to take it to different places—if you are back, placed on the axle. Leave the driving and direction to the driver of the cart. This is when backward is forward.

Youthfulness and usefulness have come to you in abundance, the abundance of the time of the former rain moderately, and he will cause to come down for you the rain, the former rain, and the latter rain in the first month (Joel 2:23). This musical reed was ready, willing, and able. When you fall in love with God, let your zeal know no bounds; never let it be cast into outer darkness (Matthew 8:12). When the Lamb of God restores us, it isn't whitewashing He whom He uses but the oil paint when using the anointing oil (Psalm 23:3, 5).

In Christ, You Have Been Made Different

It is from His bruising and brokenness that we were called and collected. As this bruised reed, you have a shed full of good and bad memories. Let your memories be your schoolteachers, and if you do, you will attain a high grade in your education.

It is from Jesus that conviction arrived as soldiers coming to a beleaguered fort. They come to relieve those who feel they have been locked in for a "fortnight"—you know, a "fort" and spending a "night" as active enemies surrounding it. It was when Christ came to seek and to save that which was lost that you realized that there were more for you, far more than those against you (Luke 10:9–10; Romans 8:31). It was Christ who disannulled everything about your style of life.

The mud wiped off the music stick, the past wiped away, cast into a pond of forgetfulness. Past mistakes are passed, dethroned so that another might sit on the throne who knew Joseph (Exodus 1:8). The shepherd realized it wasn't the reason the reed pipe recovered from its plight of the night and the dismay of the day. There were a thousand reasons why the carer of lambs should let "sleeping dogs lie." There were a million reasons why he should rescue and restore it. The more significant number, the more massive army won the day.

God Will Find and Rescue You

You may have waited many years, too many, to remember to be found and rescued and led by grace back into grace. When Christ sees us, the process isn't the exchange of one backyard in a low dwelling for another. He has something far better for you. For the bruised reed and you, there are "better" things, as found in the book of Hebrews (1:4; 6:9; 11:40). Paul used the word *better* in Philippians 1:23 and the book of Hebrews. The new status was "better" than mud and muck, better than the crushing it knew through the sheep's feet. It was "better" than the dark, long night. It was "better" than a day or days with no sunshine. Your best and blessed days are before you as you journey on with the leader, locked in his hands. The grace of God as the crook of the shepherd reaches throughout the years and takes you to Himself, found when rescued. It is when you know that "severed" is no more and that "found" becomes your foundation. The hand that grips you is no dark tunnel. It has as many promises in it as fingers on any hand and doubled in two hands. You walked out of your sorry plight, and you sang a rainbow as part of His covenant (Genesis 9:12, 16), as a bridge to freedom.

The man of the sheep rejoiced much more in finding this "reed lamb" than he would have been made happy by finding a straying sheep. We have one consolation, and that is that we can't wander beyond grace. The right hand and thine arm ... because thou hadst a favour unto them" (Psalm 44:3). You won't fall deeper than God, found and formulated to be lost no more.

You Are Going to Be the Gold of Grace

The bruised reed had been sought and found, as if a gold prospector had searched long, high, and wide but had found what he wanted. This reed was like a gold nugget. Surprisingly, it wasn't gold he found; it was just a little bit of old ore, a bruised reed that would be transformed into gold because your lover is the secret of alchemy. The alchemist always wanted to discover the secret of turning base metal into gold. The gospel you believed in the New Testament is a gospel of gold. It has the Midas touch (everything Midas touched, according to Greek legend, turned to gold).

Looking back at what has happened to you, consider this. As it is true with the music stick, so it is with you in your turmoil, mud, and feeling of darkness, when it sometimes feels as if you are in a bog of mud, left alone. It would never experience being played on the heartstrings of another, with one shepherd and several sheep as its audience. Because of this experience, you realize that in your sin, forgotten is forgiven, never to be remembered again you.

Terry Atkinson

ONE STEP BACKWARD, THREE STEPS FORWARD

Once you felt, looking backward. You took one step backward, but through the Shepherd of your soul, you take three steps forward. You had not only been forgotten but also rubbed out as if you had never existed. Don't worry, friend. You can't be rubbed out or driven out by the One who can't forget anything, yet concerning your sin, He forgets since He forgives everything.

That lost and found river reed required, as we do, a second chance, a second opportunity to perform well. Opportunity is your privilege to let God do right this time what you made a mess of last time. You were like the child with the crayon stick, scribbling on a wall and thinking you were writing the language of royalty. What should have been so good was just indelible scribbles, but then you read of the writing Pilate put over the cross of Jesus Christ (John 19:19). In the language of angels, it didn't mean what it said in Hebrew, Greek, and Latin. In their language, the interpretation of those words written above the cross of Calvary is, "I love you more than anything else in the world. Christ loved you more in depth than the oceans of the world." I will take you deeper into me than any oar dips into the water to speed a boat along. If you had to paint my love, you would soon have no paint left. It took more love, power, and grace to save you than it takes color to paint the Forth Bridge in Scotland, United Kingdom. (It is an exceptionally long bridge that takes a year to paint. When they have painted it, they commence repainting it.)

GOD HAS BROUGHT YOU FROM YOUR WORLD INTO HIS WORLD

"That is why I gave my world for your world" (John 3:16). That world of yours, which spins around like a tornado, has stopped. You are the one in the book of Acts 8:38, who asked for the chariot to stand still, just as Philip, the evangelist, spoke to the man from Ethiopia and asked it to stop because he wanted to get off. Though he had Isaiah 53 read to him, the Ethiopian man realized, as you realized, that you can move quicker in the right direction and accomplish more by walking with the conquering man, being carried and cared for, than any speeding rocket can take people to the moon. It isn't enough to speed through life. You must go through it step by step and little by little until you are made large enough to fly and not flutter, run and be weary, and walk and not faint (Isaiah 40:31).

WHAT THE ALMIGHTY HAS BROUGHT YOU INTO

Looking back, it seems as if you were better than good when you slipped out of sight into the mud, but being rescued, as a bruised reed, you would be a carbuncle or sapphire in quality. When the Lord found you going under for the third time, you who are redeemed, know that He can do better than that. For your mistakes, He will bring you to lakes of love. For your misdemeanor, He brings you to His majesty (2 Corinthians 5:21). This experience has made you realize there is no hill, not even those that surround Jerusalem, that has enough capacity to block God out of the equation. It matters little how large the dustpan or cloud the sheep created; when they move along, the Lord, God Almighty, has seen through it and reached out into it to rescue you. He became those dust particles when He became a man, as Jesus Christ, the Second Adam. The name *Adam* means "red earth" (1 Corinthians 15:45, 45).

YOU HAVE BEEN FOUND AND SAVED AT SIGNIFICANT COST

This salvation of yours, the means bringing salvation and keeping you saved, is both rich and powerful. Being saved has turned "chance" into "choice" (Jude 3:21). Your inability has become ability; like the music reed, you depend totally on your Shepherd of the sheep. You are better and cost more than "prime beef" or succulent lamb. God as the Shepherd was hungry for you. He came when no others would, and when you were hungry, He led and fed you, never accomplished without the hand of the Rescuer. The One who receives also rescues and reinstates. "You belong to Him" (1 Corinthians 6:20; 7:23).

Lifted from Deep Depths to New Heights

The best shepherds always smell of sheep; this shepherd smelled of sheep and a music flute. He lived, breathed, thought, taught, and played music. It was his passion just as you are God's. He had been christened in sweat as he sought for the lost flute. Jesus sweated great drops of blood in the garden of Gethsemane as He pleaded for you. Have you noticed the extremes of grace in these words (Luke 22:44)—"great" and "drops"? You were rescued because the Great and Good Shepherd identified with you. Remember, it doesn't matter how deep the reed slipped into the mud. It did matter if it never played another note. That meant that its talent would remain buried while it was created to send music into the man, not mud. It was created to cure loneliness and isolation.

Music has been for you a friendship bridge, which from time to time you will have to walk across. In His hands, its music can break their bands asunder and cast away their cords from us (Psalm 2:3).

Your music was lost, while the constant repetition of the sheep's call remained. You thought that in your condition you would never repaint the landscape. Over it, without help, could be written "the end." Whatever caked or covered you is gone. You required something more profound than a mudpack. You wanted the music to rise from your inside and sing your way into the heart of other people. You have attracted more people to your side through music rather than to mud, played on the slime scale of music. When called, claimed, and collected, you left the mud and your old, muddled life behind, realizing it was mud Jesus had used to heal a blind man (John 9:6). It was the New Testament writer who saw his old life as dung. He counted all things as loss (Philippians 3:7–8). You are living, loving proof that there is hope in God for the oppressed. Now in your life, there aren't the marks of sheep hooves but those of the grace of God. Believer, like the flute you are the baton that will conduct joy in the life of the men of sheep.

You Belong to Christ Jesus

Whatever shape you are found in and whatever the reason you have fallen on hard times, you still belonged to the Shepherd, remembering that when the man who lifted it took it to himself, in all its fallen nature, he loved it—warts and all. The reed, like you in your need, was rescued. It had identification with the man of the mountains and valleys. You were bruised. So was the shepherd as he sought for it (Isaiah 53:5; 2 Corinthians 5:21). You were deeply cut, as was the leader of the sheep in his searchings. His searchings are your teachings. It was covered in mud, so was the seeker who came to it (Hebrews 2:11). What identification! Pierced like a dartboard, you need to realize that just like you, so was Jesus Christ. Your past was written in mud, but your future was etched into the Rock of Ages.

Some would write across your life "forsaken" or "no hope," leaving you to die in an unmarked grave, but Jesus uses a different sort of language after He has dipped His pen in the blood of His love. The reed was pierced, so was Jesus Christ (John 19:34, 37; Zechariah 12:10). In what you are "going through"—sorry, "coming through"—Jesus Christ has "been through" the deep darkness you have suffered. He suffered on the cross when it was dark by the space of three hours (Mark 15:33). Whatever pain you feel, He has felt—touched with the feelings of our infirmities (Matthew 8:17). He can succor those who are tempted (Hebrews 2:18). The strength of the shepherd went into the weak reed. When the Bible speaks of us being "succoured" (Hebrews 2:18), it is sometimes describing the "frapping," long, strong pieces of rope that passed under a ship during a time of storm. Friend, under you are the everlasting arms. The flute never fell lower than it could be loved. If it had fallen into some disused mine, the shepherd would have faced the downhill and dark to save it.

The Shepherd Has a New Purpose for You

The leader of lambs went backward, retracing his steps so the reed was rescued. He had in his hands a new start, a new destiny for this lost, left-behind reed. He wasn't just seeking any old cylinder; he was looking for what rightly belonged to him. He would recognize it when he saw it due to the marks he had placed on it.

Whatever the man of the meadows rescued, so this music pipe was recovered for a different purpose. What has been knotty wool in your life is suddenly untangled, and from these tangles tumbles out the purposes of the Lord. It was His purposes that build an ark during a time of the flood (Genesis 6:14). It was the purpose of the Lord that opened up the Red Sea. It brought down the walls of Jericho. It is purposed as a bridge you have walked over, passing from death into life (Colossians 1:13). These purposes have made you leap for joy, higher than an Olympic high jumper would leap. Higher than the leaping of the hart. The objectives of the Lord have stood you on your feet—not to leave you standing and staring but to set you free to run the race set before you (Hebrews 12:1). What testimony is yours! No longer do you need to stand and stare at Christianity as someone window-shopping without any means to purchase or have what you see and need.

In the future, every time the King of love looks at you as a rescued, bruised reed, He thinks of the story and battle to save you, brought to His memory—fond memories. Each sheep or lamb rescued is a story from the lips of love. Every moment he handled or played the tuned tube in the future would evoke strong memories of how he had sought and found it. Every time it was played, what had been the "unfinished symphony" and the "lost cord" turned into something so new and genuine.

You who have been out of tune are now tuned in again to the shepherd's heart. The ribbon tied around the bruised tube is one of finding, rescuing, and lifting the loved from above, with a love that went beyond the pasture, quiet streams, and food laid out before enemies. The love of the keeper of sheep went deeper than mud or mine.

LOVED WITH AN IMMEASURABLE LOVE

These are all the memories of the bruised reed and you. The love of the man of the sheep was love as deep as it was high. It climbed every mountain; it forded every stream. If it meant walking the legs off his body, he did just that. Anybody else passing by this fallen architecture would pass by on the other side, for you would mean nothing to them. Others have seen you as unclean, unloved, not required—surplus to requirements. It is always remarkable how God takes what means nothing to others and brings it to Himself. It is this same God who forms diamonds from coal and pearls from pieces of raw grit. This reed, as your new life in Christ, is a signpost and a border post. The ancients always said the areas belonging to their fathers should stay (Proverbs 22:28). Ancient landmarks should remain. Nothing was wasted in Israel; even the corners of the field should be for the poor (Leviticus 19:9). The reason the lamb lover sought this stick was because he had a great love for it and wanted to reveal his character as he sought to find it. It is the believer's God. How much He loves, has loved, and will love you. These are the memories of the bruised reed. You, too, have such a glorious is your testimony.

Twelve

The Bruised Reed Found Twice

There are some couples I know who have been married twice to the same partner. They divorced but then found they couldn't live apart, so they married again. Their first marriage was all pip and no apple. Their second marriage to the same person brought the sweetness of the fruit they never saw or tasted in the first attempt. Many couples have another wedding ceremony later in life because they want to renew their vows to one another. It's sometimes the second knock of the nail, which sinks it deep into the wood, that it is going to hold things together.

God is the God of the second chance; just as this reed, we are given a second opportunity. Sometimes it is the second occasion that turns dross into gold. Need I remind you that Jesus is called the "second Adam" (1 Corinthians 15:45, 45, 47)?

It was on the second day of creation that things appeared that had never appeared on the first day (Genesis 1:6–8). Without the second day, there would have been no separating of the waters and no pathway into the third day, the day of resurrection (Acts 10:40).

There is part of rigors and experiences we wish had a second volume or the opportunity of another opportunity. We have the Second Epistle to the Corinthians, the Second Epistle to Timothy, and the Second Epistle of Peter and the Thessalonians, but we have no second epistle of the Acts of the Apostles or Romans. If we had a second book of Jonah, it might have told us how Jonah fared after his experience in Nineveh.

John Mark, like us, was given a second opportunity. He left Paul and "turned back" from the work of God. The book of Acts describes him as a "minister"; it suggests an "under-rower" (Acts 12:12; 15:37–38). He became known in the New Testament church as the "maimed thumb," because he received a second opportunity. He later wrote the Gospel of Mark.

Every time twins are born, there is a "second opportunity" presented to a family. Since having grandchildren is our opportunity to rectify the mistakes we made with our children, our children have become our schoolmasters.

In John 1:29, 36, John the Baptist had to repeat to the disciples that Jesus was the Lamb of God who would take away the sins of the world. It was after that second declaration that the believers followed Jesus to become what they would have never been but for that second opportunity.

We can see throughout the New Testament that a second visit from Paul and Silas or Paul and Barnabas strengthened the churches, taking them from just driftwood and seeing them built into glorious sailing ships of New Testament theology (Acts 18:23).

There is something rare and spectacular about anything that has come to you through much tribulation. When any two suffer together, they stand together, stay together, and perform music together (Ecclesiastes 4:9). They learn to depend wholly on each other. Where one can't be, the other can; and what one can't do, the other can. If the weak one fails or you should fall, the stronger one, the "El," will hold you up (Genesis 14:18–20, 22). When one is in need, the other ministers to that need. When the cup of one is half full, the other can fill it until it is complete and running over.

The pipe was the "act" in the Acts of the Apostles. In a more profound sense, the one who blew wind through it knew it was his very own, purchased at such a price. You cost God a double payment (1 Peter 1:18). The shepherd had become the water stalks deliverer and destiny. The music that came from it was a form of worship to its Creator. It was the reed's way of saying thank you.

You Can Function Only in His Hands

This grass pipe could function only in the hands of him who found it. Without Christ, we were just ordinary blowpipes, sometimes sending out poisonous darts as we criticized others. We can be all hot breath and nothing else. The leader and keeper found one who could take what was nothing and make it into everything. Being discovered was like a seed sown, which would grow and produce much fruit; the harvest of music was in it. After being rescued twice, it was set free. Always remember that in music, as one note follows another note, Christ follows you everywhere. "Lo, I am with you alway" (Matthew 28:20). Like a musician, He seeks to bring the best tunes of truth out of our hearts.

The reed would never be let go because it was so highly prized and priced. Not all the tea in China could buy it; the gold in the Bank of England could offer only pence. It was prized more than the paw of the bear or the head of a lion, being taken and made into a more reasonable prospect. A mere reed was a sheep guide's trophy of wonder. In it was a land not yet mapped out.

The reed pipe was his monument of success, just as you are the crystallization of the goodness of God. That reed was like the page of a book. You could read it in all it had suffered, how it had been found and reconciled to its lover and friend. The marks of life and rescue were written indelibly on it for all to see. To the sheep leader, this was his scroll of scripture.

Everything Wrong Righted

If he wanted consolation and couldn't play the instrument, he gazed at it, and the glory of the gaze entered his spirit. If he journeyed, the reed went with him. If the sheep tender lay down to sleep, it slept with him. It attended every meal. As a mirror, it reflected the shepherd's past, present, and future. He looked to the flute to finalize everything wrong, since through music, it was right. It offered to its rescuer, owner, and keeper more than any lamb, sheep, or flock of sheep. In the long nights, it could and would, with a little encouragement, speak to him in the language of love through the medium of music. The water stick was his bedtime story, for in it was the life and effort of the man who loved it enough to lift it. In it was life, and that life became the light of men (John 1:4). All these things are pure pictures of Jesus Christ. They reminded him of his victory's exploits. The things he thought couldn't happen, he suddenly, after looking upon it, realized he could do—like you, who can do all things through Christ who strengthens you (Philippians 4:13).

After being reconciled, the music stick was open to new things coming from the dexterity of its rescuer. There were unfinished melodies in that tube, as there are unfinished stories in your life, written not on a computer disc but in books and in the lives of others (John 21:25). As the pipe influenced others, so will you. It was rescued, not to continue to bleat as a rescued sheep but to do something different. Every day was a new miracle; the original came out of the old (2 Corinthians 5:17–18). The reed brought that regal to the fore when rescued. The instrument would never soar like an eagle, but it could produce that higher than the eagle in any performance, and it was more than a concert; it was praise. It would show forth the praises of him whom it was connected to (1 Peter 2:9).

Pebbles Can Become Pearls

Suppose it was "water music" that could be played on the hollow vehicle because it had been there. There could be depths sounding from it because that was its experience. It hadn't been taught music from a book, but the author of its music had trained it. The hours of deep suffering were part of it because of its experience. If a drowning man wanted the music to help him learn to swim, he could turn to the flute, because it had been there. Emerging from what it had fallen into, pearls with gems appeared in the sound of its music.

Not just played with a mere toy, it was in a concert with its finder. Regular service wouldn't be resumed. The ribbed instrument had a twinkle in every note borrowed from the night sky as it lay in the sludge and struggle of a long night. Music was usual for a reed, but this pipe had had music forced into its heart through suffering. After its experience, it was no longer just a musical reed; it was an instrument with ability; the inability had gone. Where it had just sounded out music, it could now play its way into the heart. It could melt clouds into the sunshine, and swollen rivers of fear and doubt as a King Canute (the king who believed the tide would stop coming in if he commanded it) would remain static and know the power of a restraining hand. Because this reed knew its place in the hands of the shepherd, it was able to command other things into their correct order, like musical notes on the scales.

It was this music that turned every lamb into a sheep. It turned sweet stream water into wine. It had the capability of seeing change when others saw only decay. It transformed the growl of the bear into a welcoming party. The king of the jungle was dethroned by a reed of music that had become the pipe of peace.

The Pipe Became a Pipe of Peace

If it was the music of the melancholy, it was equal to that, for this was its testimony. There was a meager requirement for the leader of lambs to pull himself up by his shoelaces. If the player required the music of sorrow, here was the vehicle. If it was the mood of peace as they walked by "still" waters, waters of "quietness" (Psalm 23:2), here was the channel of peace.

Just by being there and feeling the touch of the sheep gatherer's hand, the reed felt at peace. All was well when it was taken and used to turn the storm into calm and hurt into happiness. The rescued reed was the child of the second touch, the added touching of its finder. "Finders are keepers" is an old English proverb.

GOD CARES FOR YOU AS IF YOU ARE HIS ONLY CHILD

Believer, you are capable of such a range of music, because of your experience in God. You might not be of a musical disposition, but you aren't graceless. Most musical instruments require tuning from time to time. They must be pitch perfect sometimes. Retuned every time we come before the Lord, we are still in His stillness (Psalm 46:10). "Be still and know that I am God." "Let go and let God." There is a phrase "resting the instrument." This isn't because it is tired but I guess it's to give the instrumentalist time to get his second wind. It was a second wind, a second chance, a second opportunity this flute was experiencing. The Japanese nation has a saying: "slowing down, to let the soul catch up with the body." Hence the translation of Psalm 23:1: "The Lord is my pacesetter." It would seem as if the flute was laid aside to let its music catch up with it. The horse and the rider, who are separated, are going nowhere.

Your triumphant rescue was because of truth, the whole truth; what God loves He cherishes, and He cares for you like no other. "Whole truth" heals into "wholeness." Having rescued one pipe, the shepherd had only one tube of music to love. He could give it all his attention, as if in a flock of sheep this was the only sheep. The sun in the blue sky shines on the one apple as if it were the only apple that ever lived and grew. That is how God loves you (Psalm 17:8) being away from the shepherd's heartbeat. Bind him hand and foot, take him away, and cast him into outer darkness (Matthew 22:13) were all notes in each recital. The reed had been christened in sorrow, baptized in joy, and brought to the beginning of what seemed to be an end. Metaphorically this instrument of worship and wonder had been through both the Red Sea and the River Jordan.

The shepherd was thinking and redesigning the reed as God had put His design into creating the world. Elohim marked every leaf with lines, and He arranged the color and contour of every flower (Genesis 1:1–10). It was more impressive than exceptional. It was one of a kind, the shepherd kind, for it was his kindness. It had taken such an endeavor to rescue it.

There Is Great Rejoicing When the Prodigal Returns

The pipe reed was more desirable than song or wine, night fire or firefly. This prodigal was better for him than many flocks of sheep. It could do what they collectively or individually could never do. It could take him places as he marched in time to the music. The difference between the reed and the sheep was that the sheep always needed leading. Its greatness was in its vulnerability everywhere, but it dispensed its reward, in that it could bring the human spirit into realms never entered. It went boldly where no man had ever gone before. One note of music was a giant step for this shepherd as he faced an uphill battle.

Being "twice bought" proved twice as useful. Twice visited, it knew something of the warmth and capacity or incapability of a second chance.

It was closer to the sheep leader than any newborn lamb. It was more and more. More selected than the timbral and the dance. It was more acceptable than the finest of the wheat, more refined than the gold of Ophir. Better than Goliath's sword. That sword never produced a single note of music. It brought more rejoicing than at the time of the harvest or sheep sales. It combined every musical sound in the heart of the shepherd and then released it to do its healing work. The sound of the trumpet hidden in each musical note was silver. The ram's horn was part of its variety. The sound was that of being brought to the shepherd twice. For the tube, it was only the second rung in the ladder of escape. More rungs were added for ascension. It could sound a warning as well as a welcome. It could sound out a word of command: go or come. It was higher than any mountain peak. It was more to his heart of love than the psaltery and harp. It could achieve more than a stringed instrument or brass section. The organ was left in the shade when this came into the glory of its music. As a wind instrument, it was bought twice so that it could blow away all torments and times of tragedy. Just as it was dependent on the wind blowing through it, so are we dependent on Jesus Christ (John 3:8).

Each performance was one of expressing thankfulness and meaningfulness to all it met. It was like the Christian forgiven who wanted to forgive everybody it met. It was the experience as if it had swallowed sunshine.

THE EXPANSE OF THE REED WAS GREATER

It could sound out in the minor or primary key. The harmony of it became a cord, taken from the word *accord*, meaning "one" (Acts 2:1). A little gift of nature in the form of a reed would become one with the shepherd—greatness and smallness, joined at the hip through bruising, one with the shepherd, one with nature. It was one with the universe. Little wonder that its music was lined with silver mined from deep mines. Reclaimed, it meant that it was more than a second glance in a mirror; this would be a permanent picture.

The pastoral reed, having been rescued, was a witness under the oath of death to tell the truth, the whole truth, and nothing but the truth. (The oath was taken in an English court as one swears on the Bible.) Each note, song, or melody was a witness to others of it being rescued and restored.

Terry Atkinson

SUFFERING PROCURES HOLINESS AND ONENESS

Here was the low and high cymbal. Only this reed could make music better and longer lasting than any instrument ever created.

When bought twice, it felt the touch of his hand, not a new hand but an old hand with a new contact. We sometimes forget that from violin to viola, each instrument basked into shape. The golden candlestick from the Tabernacle was beaten from one piece (Exodus 25:31–35). The hammer blows in this reed were converted into music.

The pipe was above all others because it had fallen below them when it was lost. Christ in His exaltation is far above others because He went lower than any man in His sufferings (Philippians 2:9); what it suffered as a hollow pipe it used to make it into a conduit of peace.

The music sounding out meant that what the pastor couldn't express in mere words, deeds, thoughts or through his creative ability, he communicated through this reed. It was like those the Spirit of God anointed in Acts 2:4, who spoke in another language. It is the language of the broken heart. Just as in Acts 2:4, music speaks all the languages of the world. If you require a word for your broken world or a word when your words can't form properly, the reed made pronouncements.

It sometimes hurts so much to pay for a thing twice; mainly if you do so, your hand reaches the bottom of your pocket. Jesus emptied Himself for you (Philippians 2:6–9), the self-emptying of Christ, so you might empty yourself in that area He reserved for you. He was the shepherd, since our Jesus never ran out of patience. Each of your problems was dealt with as the music stick was dealt with twice. Once by you, but you fell into slime and soot. Then after being dealt with a second time, you were raised, as white as flour.

As in your life, each note was an expression of deep love and thankfulness. The hurt it had experienced now clothed every musical note. Every time it was played, it reflected the glory of the shepherd, who rescued it and passed through much sorrow to bring joy unspeakable and full of glory into it (1 Peter 1:8). Each time you worship, it is your way of saying, "Thank you for coming a second time to rescue me."

Thirteen

The Bruised Reed Grew through Suffering

We now come to the cream and crux of the bruised reed. Suffering is something we all experience, and it matters to us to understand its depth, height, breadth, and length. To comprehend it is an outstanding achievement, and it forges a medal in your heart. It is the "well" of the words "well done!" As you place in the balances all that happened to the bruised reed, you will see that the massive things were those things it suffered while away from the shepherd's side while in Ruin Ravine. To have a full-star night and a bright moon means you will see as a shroud the blackness of the night. The moon and stars come into the blackest of nights, held in place as if they are proving a balance for us in our midnight drama.

They were continuing to fulfill their dreams, while the reed wasn't enjoying this nightmare. There was no soft pillow here. There was none to call upon in the day of calamity. Like a sinking ship, it had gone to the bottom.

The suffering of the bruised reed was no darkened moment, seized upon by highwaymen. The reed was suffering a misdemeanor, since it was lost. It was the moment of toasting the rejoicing when found. The flag found was like the discovery of a new continent. The reed had been to school, Saint Mary's, at the feet of Jesus

(John 11:20, 32; Luke 10:39). It had visited the carpenter's bench in Nazareth, feeling the cutting blade that made it into an instrument of praise and worship. In a figure of speech, it had carried the cross of Christ while bogged down in mud and mire. It came up smelling of more than roses; it was able to play the music that was more appreciated than roses. The dandelion was a rare flower of exquisite beauty. The nails of disappointment and rejection hammered into it held it fast. More in depth than that, those nails of steel were taken and translated into music. Anything that is going to last forever must have a forever experience that takes it to the local duck pond and unceremoniously sees it baptized, sitting on a ducking stool.

SUFFERING PUTS MUSIC INTO OUR SOULS

Mary tried to gain musical excellence three times. This was Mary's fourth attempt. It mattered that she should pass the grade this time, because a future occupation hung from her ability to play and join the British Northern Light Orchestra. Her father knew Mary had failed to reach the grade when he saw her face. Mary had gone in as a sunbeam and came out of the auditorium, looking like a frog with its marked face of frowning. The director of music called Mary's father onside. He explained, "Your daughter will never reach the highest grade until her heart is broken and healed. The lady is musically perfect; she hits the right notes. Your daughter is note perfect, but I want some deep expression in her musical ability. But she lacks empathy to express the music from her heart."

Six months later, her boyfriend left her; her grandfather died suddenly. Mary was forlorn because of her loss. Her heart, hammered into small pieces, just fell apart. She had been deeply in love. Grandfather had been her stalwart. Another three months passed, and Mary, the family rose, had to retake the vital music grade. "Would she fail again?" That was the question everybody was asking. Mary, broken in heart, continued practicing, but something had happened to her that reached the sides, top, and bottom of her heart. The musical examination was now complete, and she passed it with a top grade. The secret was, she was bruised, and through that hurt came the passion of perfection Mary had lacked. This daughter not only played music; she felt it in her soul.

The pipe music had been tucked into the shepherd's attire; all seemed well. Life was easy and breezy. But its moments of glory had to be extended through the things it would suffer. Dr. Mud is a great music teacher. There is an academy where bruises and more bruises acclaim the achievements. Its most remarkable attribute, like yours, is that you have suffered. After ye have suffered a while, make you perfect, stablish, strengthen, settle you (1 Peter 5:10).

By the side of the river, the scenes were as continuous as the experiences—the same day on day, a night on night. The river always flowed by. The birds of the air always flew over it. Everything was out of reach for one with no hands. There had to be something more to life than this. It could grow only into what nature determined as it grew by the riverside. That natural needs the introduction of the spiritual for it to mean anything in this life. It must contain a message of hope, for this flute plays the music of hope, deep and pure.

You Mature through What You Suffer

The reed, like you, learned more in five minutes of being lost in loads of rubbish than it would have learned in fifty years by the river on a Sunday afternoon. Where it fell was no place for punting. You will learn far more when wrestling against the world, flesh, and the devil than you will ever know while sitting in a pew on a Sunday morning. We all must learn, as the disciples did, to get out of the boat (Mark 5:2). Like the goods displayed in the shop window, we all look so good; we are all equal. It is the buying and wearing of them that puts them to the test. It is when our feet touch the floor that we determine whether they were worth the price. You were worth saving because the price paid wasn't silver or gold (1 Peter 1:18–19). It was "precious" (unequalled) blood that ransomed and restored you.

There are some sweet experiences outside of God, but they are sticky, messy, and shallow; and as summer migrants, they soon disappear. They fly away as bird visitors, which are just here for the summer. Other tough troubles are of "anvil quality" and bind your spirit with hoops of steel. Mountains aren't swept away by a zephyr. The pipe was wounded and winded before it could mean more than the normal.

WE ARE OFTEN KNOCKED DOWN BUT NOT KNOCKED OUT

There must be poundings of the soul we must all endure. We shall be "knocked down but not knocked out" (J. B. Phillips translation of 2 Corinthians 4:8). Being knocked out of shape, we lose our way. What was a spring day and a summer's festival become a valley of despair. It is most difficult to form shapes from material that resists you. Have you tried bending steel with your two hands? That is why you cost Christ so much on the cross. Within what we suffer are rare qualities of character added to us. Seeing the jewelry that costs a lot, we can only stare at the jeweler's window display. To obtain it, we must buy it or become a lapidary and shape it. There are things more precious than silver or gold, which must be added to our character so we live the divine nature.

Suffering breaks us open, and as we open, there is the heralding of a new dawn. It is only when the flower petals open that the bee is busy making honey. The plowed field can then receive the seeds of a new harvest of hope. Pain can be so painful until we discover what it is telling us. Every pain can be a warning of something more difficult to follow. Find in your pain a new plan or panacea for your ills. These are some of the lessons the pipe learned while lying on the ground, hurt, hapless, and hopeless.

At last, it was unfettered, but in that experience, it found far more shackles than it had ever known while resting in the palm of the sheep keeper. It was like a sheep to the slaughterhouse and then onto the butcher's bench. Remember, it fell in the place of the scattered bones, Ruin Ravine.

Each thing the tube suffered was like a signpost that pointed to the right way. We can read in the reed all we need when we bleed. The musical instrument was left for a few days so it might find new expressions of music and feel the warmth of the hand of the music maestro again and again, left lost in the cold so it might find a new warmth in its music. Feeling no hand around or upon it, the mud and such offered no gentle squeeze.

You Are Now Being Pieced Together Like a Jigsaw

We are going to be "masterpieces" (Ephesians 2:10). From the mud in which He found us in, when we couldn't swim through the mess that was around us, from that mud, He brings many colors for our character, as colorful as any rainbow (1 Peter 4:10; Ephesians 2:1). You know, if you throw a stone into muddy water, in the splash, it makes many colors appear.

The masterpiece of God's creation is worth the brush strokes and the knife used in oil paintings. The brush strokes are sometimes heavy. The oil paint is scraped off and onto the canvass. Now we are being pieced together by the Shepherd's nail-pierced hands. The cutting edge, that edgy spirit, is sometimes withdrawn like a bad tooth. That short temper is having its fuse lengthened. The rebellion in us is being routed and redirected. That rushing in where angels fear to tread is enlarged so we don't rush into situations and make them worse. We know the difference between the "bull and the China shop" mentality. The sour notes in this reed were left to die.

That rescuer's hand became the repair shop. That which was

crushed, hurt, and misplaced would soon be normalized, and that malfunctioning would be adjusted.

The pastoral instrument wasn't found and made into the perfect tool. There was still a lot of work to do. It would take dexterity of those fingers, which had helped to birth lambs and conquer bears and lions and had worked as a weaver with wool, to form an exquisite pattern in coarse material. There wouldn't be the coarse strength used when fighting a wild animal used. It would be a "hand as iron in a velvet glove" approach. The ranges of its music had to increase. The notes that couldn't sound would be. Those notes that didn't sound right were adjusted. Something had to happen to it for the miracle of developing nature had to be part of it. The same, safe hands that helped and held the reed could be gentle when delivering spring lambs.

CHRIST, THE SHEPHERD, CAN BE ABSENT

While the reed was quickly lost, it was never really lost until the leader of lambs stopped looking for it. In Luke 2:46, Mary and Joseph traveled for one day without missing the presence of Jesus. It then took three days to find Him. Worse than being lost is to be missing and not to matter. It is indeed an awful lot if I could be last when you have passed; that would be an awful lot. The all-seeing eye sees you. The all-strong hand lifts you—not to be the same as you were but to make a success out of your failure.

When deep down in the mud of our thinking, we miss the breath of the music Creator. We can't play one day without His inward breathing. Lost to Him, we are lost to everything.

In John 3:16, when the word *perish* is used, it can mean "to be out of circulation." The dime or the dollar, the pound or the penny, is worth the same when lost. It is the midnight hour followed by the dawn of day. What was wrong would be put right, right on time, and at the right moment, bringing peace and purpose to the pipe.

Nothing would happen to it that couldn't be taken and used. The dung could grow roses. The clay from it would appear in the potter's vessel. From the black soil, a diamond arrived in the form of a qualified music stick, followed by many songs that were of diamond quality. The mud could and would contain gems.

When I see white milk come from brown cows, which eat golden hay and green grass, I am amazed. The darkness contained voices of hope and renewal. Each time it felt the tread of a hoof on it, it was being stamped, not in the image of a sheep but in the image of the shepherd, for it would express his glory as he played it.

Avoid Sorrow by Converting It

Whatever you do, don't surround yourself with your sorrows, for if you do, you will find that it is a woollen shawl you are wearing. A small thread is hanging down, and if it gets caught on any thorny branch, the whole garment is unceremoniously unraveled. If all you do is surround yourself with sorrowful people, you will never see a rainbow in your sky. No man or woman who has lost the egg and spoon race beats himself or herself with the spoon. Rather than having that encounter with mud, which can soon be unraveled or washed away, have such an enrichment of God that can't fail. The dullest moment can be the greatest. Let that dull thud as you fall become a trumpet, a rallying call to your spirit, to let Him lift you into the land of going on.

It isn't where or how you fall. It isn't where you land that matters. The important thing is that the Carpenter-cum-Shepherd of Nazareth finds you with His bag of carpenter's tools. Don't stay there; let the hand that beckons take hold of you, for all things were in the hands of the sheep lover. Let that place of surrender, that place of dark mud, become the place where change begins, where you find decay. The tune player didn't mind the worms or slugs as he sought for his best friend. Dirt meant duty to him. His attention is always on you.

Languish Converted through Laughter

If the reed had stayed at the shepherd's side forever, its future, vision, and ability would have been limited. Dull as dishwater, music was just a meander. Flat tones and sad echoes are coming from the tube. The slightest rub or knock, a sheep rushing by, or a shepherd rushing to the aid of a sick sheep could jolt it out of tune. Let the great Shepherd sanctify your moments of sheer terror and turn them into the laughter expressed when something valuable appears, taking the earth that surrounds the fallen reed, sweeping it away as if the walls of Jericho had fallen away.

The finder is the keeper; that can and will start again. Being found is like being brought back to the beginning of the race you have just lost. This time you become a born winner. The born loser is converted. He commences turning a page of grace to begin again where it fell. He lifts you from being grounded to being found in hope, love, faith, and joy. The moments we spend when we feel we have been left alone—that loneliness, helplessness, and the emptiness of the sheep's scout filling us—become the particles of our most outstanding achievements.

Having Been Useless, You Can Be Useful

The pasture man had found the reed battered, mudded, and bruised. It was now just a useless thing. The guide of the sheep didn't let that become its graveyard or scrapyard. His theology is never dead and buried, therefore forgotten. If the leader has lost one of his heartstrings, he must seek until he finds it, for without it he would be incomplete. His would be slumbering cords and silent notes.

In the eyes of both sheep and keeper, the fallen pipe wasn't worth anything. This pastoral feature was his paradise on earth.

Lovingly the sheep shearer lifts it and washes, turning it this way and that, handled like the first prize at a show. Rectifying the position of the mouth reed, he blows on it with his breath and begins to play it. After a few more pierced holes and reconstruction, the pigsty becomes a palace. The tube of music is an orchestra, a one-man band. The reed becomes a symphony in harmony with the master of music.

You Can Enter into New Heights from Deep Depths

It will do for the master what the keeper has done for it. It will lift him into new heights. It will help him to overcome all things. It will lift him higher than any mountain peak. It will take him through every valley and skip him across any swollen stream. It will be as any instrument is to the instrumentalist, your faithful servant. Unlike Cain, it is its brother's keeper (Genesis 4:9).

This story of the bruised reed is your account. It is my story, your story, that becomes your song, day and dusk, night and needy. Therefore, sometimes we must suffer to bring out the depths of our hearts. Cream and cheese are produced, along with butter by churning, and we are made by the constant turnings of life, which seem to leave us in a spin. The wonderful thing is that the music is now more in depth; you can hear the dulcet tones. It reaches, in the hands of the leader, deeper depths and can reach higher heights than it could have ever done before. He nearly must invent a different musical scale for it. The music stick could now get to the top without climbing a ladder. It could go to new depths without falling. It played its way from one extreme to the other. It was so inspiring; the trees of the fields clapped their hands. The river went quiet, so a greater volume of music trilled along the pathway. It was taken from being "left" to being "lifted," and love did it all. This was the spirit of the master of music. His desire sprang into action as the music sounded, and birds stopped their dawn chorus to listen—held spellbound by a new sound in the universe.

GOD WANTS TO DRAW NEW PATTERNS IN YOUR LIFE

In the mud, the foot of the bear or lion has done its crushing, crashing work. The rains had come to wash it away forever, snatched away on a flood. The winds wanted to roll it as a barrel down a steep hill, and as it descended, it would go into a deep valley from a sheer cliff drop. Feet and claws had pounded it but not destroyed it. Something from their wild nature entered it. What might have been a chocolate solder became a bodyguard of steel, a fully clad Roman soldier (Ephesians 6:11, 13).

The marks found on it, after it is lifted by the hand of the lamb leader, aren't the shape or prints of the lion's paw or the sheep's foot, but they are the patterns of glory, the glory of being sought, found, and loved.

The suffering has become an artist and potter with the pastoral reed. The things we suffer become our tuning fork. There is room here for the treble voice, the baritone, tenor, and contralto. It is both operatic and dynamic. The bruising has enlarged and engaged the range of the thin pipe and turned it into an orchestra, a symphony. Is it not the organ you have to tread on and then push its stops? Isn't it the drum you have to beat? The cymbals you must crash. It is the harp you pluck. For pure music on the piano, you must press notes and send hammers crashing into taught wires. The suffering it has passed through has worked wonders. There is such a range in its capabilities that would never have been there without the bruising. You can now understand what the Bible means when it says, "A bruised reed shall He not break" (Matthew 12:20).

Fourteen

The Reed Bruised but Victorious

M aybe the title of this chapter should be "The Limp of Victory." When we go through any period of suffering, such as the bruised reed, it might leave us feeling like we should be robust, strong, and unassailable. If that is how you think, then you have missed the whole teaching of the bruised reed. Maybe, just maybe, you think this chapter should be "The Leap, Laugh, or Lap of Victory." Don't you mean the sheer joy of victory? We should be describing the feeling of the football player when he handles the FA Cup (English Football Association) as the winning captain or when an American team wins their baseball final. It would be nicer than a sweet orange if that were true, but sometimes the opposite is the truth. There are experiences, such as the bruised reed had, that leave us broken, bleeding, and dying.

Should the chapter title reflect success and not limping along? Will suffering produce Limp Along Lesleys? We should be meditating on emptying the full cup of wine, just as they did after a successful encounter, and winning against the odds in a Greek marathon. (This describes the ceremony of any Greek athlete after winning a race. He emptied a cup of wine as an offering to his god.) Maybe we should write about the laurel leaf of success. (These were given to the successful runner or anyone who fought and won.) The chapter title still stands as it is because lots of people have a limp that reminds them of their encounter with suffering, bringing them into the realm of the bruised reed that wasn't broken. If you ask some people about their operation, they will roll up their trouser leg or lift their sleeve and reveal an enormous scar; and when they do, the conversation concludes, because the scars are their spokesperson.

Many a successful football, baseball, or cricket team, declared winners by a mile, carry deep bruises with them, only seen in the shower they take after they have fought a good fight. These bruises become their medals. How often have you met a child who had fallen? And to prove the mishap, they wanted you to see their wounds. These children add sticking plaster just to emphasize what has happened to them.

A Disability Can Be an Ability

In Genesis 32:25, 31–32, Jacob walked with a limp, but that limp was a sign. It was God's signature of his spirituality. The human capability of Jacob was restricted. In that restriction, you see beams of glory in the word *prince*. The bruised reed was left with marks on it so all who examined it might understand why it was bruised. That bruising didn't limit it but set it free, as we discussed earlier in this book.

If you fall, for whatever reason, you are going to get hurt. That hurt doesn't need to become self-pity but a spur to move you into more profound things for God. The fee for joining a self-pity club is self-pity. If you are knocked down deeper than depth, grab some of the precious diamonds and sapphires of life. At the same time you are descending, grab some of the wood of the shaft of the mine—not to use as a crutch but as a plank to sail into any harbor after a great storm. Better still, obtain the materials for an ark to meet another storm greater than you have ever experienced. In one storm, you will always find the driftwood to build another boat.

There are enough highly organized self-pity clubs without

you becoming a member. Acts of grace aren't only ours when we need them. They are there all the time, but being strong and self-assertive, we don't believe we have them. We are self-sufficient and self-assertive.

GOD ALLOWS SUFFERING SO YOU CAN DISCOVER WHO HE IS

Jacob called the name of the place where his thigh was displaced Penile, which means "the face of God" (Genesis 32:30). We are told so much about the love of God, but few ever mention the sufferings of God. In every pain, there is the face of God if you look for it. Suffering seems to have been the adage of God for Jacob. Always see what is more profound than the suffering; see beyond the cutting knife and gaze into the healing. See whose face is above the blade. On the altar Isaac could have overcome his father, Abraham, but he didn't; he fully surrendered under the knife (Genesis 22:9–10).

GOD ALLOWS ALL THINGS FOR YOUR DEVELOPMENT

Can you see the suffering face of Christ reflected in another's suffering? Can you believe that the sufferings of Christ are seen reflected in your sufferings? Suffering in the form of chains that bind you but wings you can use to fly into any sphere. It will bring you into the area of the bruised reed. Never would Jacob again run away or ahead of God. He had a life of catching up. The thigh out of joint was God's means of slowing him down (Genesis 32:25, 31–32). He was so slow that the Lord could catch up with him and walk and talk with him. The sheep leader certainly caught up with the bruised reed when it fell into its surroundings, and they overwhelmed it.

God doesn't always—in fact, maybe never—use His fists to chastise us. He used the hoofs of the sheep and the mud with chips of rock to accomplish His design for the bruised reed. When the sheep saw and heard the rocks in the valley falling, they moved nearer the shepherd for safety. They would never accuse the sheep leader of bad management.

The valley and the deep dell are our playmates in this life. God doesn't allow us to suffer, just as the sheep leader didn't allow the music stalk to suffer to get it at demand or destroy. You can suffer so that you might get a better picture of the Almighty. Within the pain, there is a reign, the reign of the eternal. As the archer has a thousand arrows, Jehovah has a million ways to deal with us in our rebellion and stupidity. When the mirror is dirty, it reflects an image that isn't true. For it to reflect what is nearest to it, it must be wiped with a duster or any old rag. It sometimes takes much rubbing and drubbing before it reflects that correct reflection.

Suffering brings you to your lowest ebb. It is when the boat can't sail, the tide is out, and you have to trust the Lord to bring the tide in. If you make any sea journey, you will get the taste of salt in your spit. It was when the Lord made the whale sick that it coughed up Jonah.

SUFFERING IDENTIFIES YOU WITH CHRIST

If you're suffering, you can sometimes feel the nails driven into your hands and feet. You feel the thorns pushed into your brow. The whiplashes are yours. There is a valid identification with Christ. It was the reed lost that identified it with the suffering and caring, knowing, and leading shepherd. Our suffering is but sour wine compared to His vinegar suffering. The Greek liturgy, referring to Christ's suffering, says, "Thine unknown sufferings."

Those in the Commonwealth Games get gold, silver, and bronze medals. The only medal or medallion the apostle Paul received in his body were the marks of the Lord Jesus Christ (Galatians 6:17).

Terry Atkinson

Suffering Can Give You Ability

It was that suffering that taught Jacob to "prevail," "to be able" (Genesis 32:25, 28). How do you know whether you are able? It means that in all your suffering, you are more than able to bear it. "We are more than conquerors through him that loved us" (Romans 8:37).

British goods have a kitemark placed on them, stating that the good have been tested and will remain firm under pressure. We need the kitemark of the kiss of Jesus on our lives; it will speak volumes of our capabilities because of Christ. The kitemark means "tried and tested." The marks on your character mean you have not only "entered suffering" but also have come out on the other side larger and better equipped to deal with life's sharp stones.

The other side of the coin for Jacob was the face of Jehovah with suffering on the other side. Let the beam of His glory and smile shine in your suffering. Each note played by the tuner was a reflection after suffering of his character. It said to all who saw the reed, "My master is capable." We will never be able to determine why El Shaddai has arranged this. Can suffering be part of that arrangement? Shall you not drink from the same cup as Jesus Christ (Matthew 20:22)? "Thine unknown sufferings" (part of the Greek liturgy) means we can never fathom what He suffered. No word or words in English, French, or German dictionaries can explain it.

If you want scent, you crush flowers and herbs. If you want squash, you crush an orange. Crush an apple, and you have sweet cider. If you desire wine, you crush a grape. How good it is to smell a bowl of crushed heather. Olives are crushed for the oil. Nobody thinks of the pain of the crushing. The same applies to remove gold and silver from ore—the process demands crushing and a fire.

IN THIS WARFARE, YOU WILL GET WOUNDED

If you think every victory brings you through every experience without a limp, scare, or wound, think again. The reed was bruised and battered but was never unloved or unsought. It is the hammering of the nail that makes the peg or wood hold strong. There are times when we wrestle with the Immortal, but the Lord always prevails, yet in a sense we prevail because we find the strength to go on believing. That hip out of joint limited Jacob from running away from God and going his own way. It is better to hobble after the Lord than to run away in sin. The bruised reed had fallen from the shepherd's side, and that fall added another color to it. The "manifold" grace of God, the many-colored grace of God, was seen in it as part of the bruising (1 Peter 4:10).

DON'T LET A LIMP LIMIT YOU

You limp, you have pain, you have a disorder, but you travel on. The attitude of the bruised pipe wasn't one of "I have suffered; therefore, I am limited." Meet some of the people in the world who have suffered. In different wars, having faculties blown from their body, they still smile; they always cheer. These warriors don't give in. They even contribute to humanity. When the cup was empty, because they had a full cup of wine after winning the race, they broke the cup. (It was the ceremony when the Greek runner won a race.) It was through the crack in this vessel that the rising sun shone. Be reminded in one of the Greek marathons that it wasn't the first past the post who was the winner but the one who was going over the line, whose torch was still burning. There is so much "light" in our "light" affliction (2 Corinthians 4:17). That light will see you through every valley and take you over every mountain.

Terry Atkinson

Our Dark and Dreary Afflictions Become Torch Holders for "Light"

"For our light affliction, which is but for a moment worketh for us a far more exceeding and eternal weight of glory." This is a greater multiplication of glory, the glory of the nature of Jesus Christ (2 Corinthians 4:17). It is our "light," "feathery" afflictions that result in pure gold being deposited in earthen vessels of clay. The bruising of the reed of music was nothing compared to the beautiful music it produced when it played, then blown.

God Changes Us Within

The last time we read something about Jacob is during the sunset of his life (Genesis 28:11). His adventure was over. It never arose again until he had wrestled with the invisible and prevailed, and had his name changed from "twister" (so twisted he would have made a good bottle opener) and "cunning" to a "prince" with God (Genesis 32:31). It was a prince at a price. Since it is the king as part of a kingdom, never have one without the other. All this is relative to the bruised reed as it hit the ravine floor.

The English meaning of *prevail* is to be "above others." The Hebrew meaning is "to be able" (Genesis 32:25). His spirituality began from this moment. God, give me a limp! God not only provides some things, but He also allows them to happen, so that through that happening, you can find happiness. I know it is a blessing in disguise, but it is well disguised.

There was a lady in one church I pastored who had only one hand. With one hand missing, she was never missing. With her hand removed, she did more than an army of able-bodied people. The woman was always the first in the queue if I wanted work done in the church. If I wished for help, she gave it with one hand, which was as good as three hands. Infirmity doesn't mean incapacity. When we suffer, we illustrate what we mean by the "limp of suffering."

There Is a Price We All Pay

A price had to be paid for that victory. Part of Jacob's body suffered. If you don't believe in the "Limp of Victory," watch soldiers who return while wounded, limping, hobbling, being wheeled, or carried on a stretcher. Observe soldiers coming from any war, and see some of them limp home, but they have won.

The price was paid by the flute when it was mudded and lost. It was the price of glorious music. What happened to it made it complete.

During my lifetime I have met many people with one hand, and with one hand they have caught what life threw at them. They caught it and reformed it into something else. Having met with people with one leg, I have been a witness to them kicking back with one leg, even scoring more goals with one leg than some would ever score if they had the legs of a centipede. With one leg and one foot, they have kicked depression and self-pity into oblivion. Some stand better and more equally balanced on one leg than on two.

Maurice Boyle, the blind preacher, told me, "I have led so many people to the Lord and influenced so many through my preaching since I became blind. I seem to have a deeper and wider vision of my calling." There are those with one eye who have a far grander vision. They receive something and are given the proverbial "full of eyes within and without." Some have only one arm, but that arm has held and helped so many other people in their distress. That one arm has become a vine with many branches. They are ever available, ready, willing, and able to let you lean on that one arm, just as John leaned on the breast of Jesus at the Last Supper (John 21:20). He never wore his heart on his sleeve since if he had only one arm, and he needed that to keep himself free from sentiment.

Some have suffered who can't give you a hand because they have lost it, but they can and do put their shoulder to the wheel. In losing faculty, we can gain many things. People who have suffered will attract suffering people. There was that smiling Christian with fingers missing from one hand who could handle money swifter and more deliberately than a weaver's shuttle. When he shook your hand, it was like experiencing a hole in one.

Not All Medals Decorate the Chest

Have a look at one of the ships returning from war, with the deck all shot up and the main guns blasted off its deck. No lifeboats are intact. The ship's railings are missing, as if it is just a floating plank. The flag of the nation has been uprooted from its pole and tossed into the sea like a spear thrown. That ship carries the pride of a nation with it.

In any storm, we must learn to roll with the ship. Every scar was and is a medal, not given by others but received during the conflict. Carrying suffering like soldiers means you have already received your recognition. These bruises and torn flesh are your real medals. You have been bloodied but not bowed. It isn't the war that determines what we are but how we suffer and what our capabilities are after we have suffered.

There Are Blessings in Bruising

See that wounded soldier stepping off the ship that brought him home. You will see blindness, deafness, suffering on a colossal scale, but those are part of their victory. You would begin to wonder what sort of war these soldiers fought if every returning soldier was able bodied, smartly dressed, and clean shaven. Nobody is walking with the aid of sticks and sitting in wheelchairs.

In my book *In Sickness and in Health*, there is a chapter on "The

Blessings of Bruising." There should be a long chapter in everybody's life on the things they have suffered because the person took a stand. If you take your stand for Christ, you are going to become a target. Targets struck many times have many holes in their surface where an arrow or bullet has penetrated.

CIRCUMSTANCES CAN BRUISE US

The bruised reed was cared for and collected by the hand of the shepherd. It was the impact when it hit the ground, and the surrounding sheep's hoofs pounding it told you where it had been. That fall, flung, knocked the old music out of it to make way for a new melody. Like us, it had been through the school of hard knocks. These knocks don't take the stuffing out of us, since they never took the music out of the reed. In the mud and suffering, there are steel ingots we all need if we are going to climb high after being so low. If you are going to climb every mountain, you must go through every valley. Whatever the amount or how you suffer, don't lose your identity. However bent or bruised the reed was, it remained what it was. Its potential was buried for a while but not dead and buried. Buried talents are still talents, even when buried. For the bruised stick, its best days were before it, as if a page had been turned in its Book of Life.

LEARNING TO LIVE IN VICTORY MEANS A BATTLE

Prince Harry of the English royal family, the grandson of Queen Elizabeth II, has done much to promote the Invictus Games. You may have seen the Invictus Games, where the contestants have paraplegia. The word *invictus* means "in victory," taken from the poem by William Ernest Henley. It suggests those "unconquerable." They wouldn't give in; they didn't know what the word *defeat* meant. Nobody had told them they should shut up shop when they were injured and lay down to die. They are undefeated. After multiple operations, they exhibit resurrection life through their sufferings (Philippians 3:10). Something is a "tragedy" only if you let it defeat you and produce an evil spirit. "Tragedy" suggests something out of control.

Here is a line from the original poem of that name, "Invictus": "Bloody but unbowed," author William Ernest Henley wrote. If they want to know how you fought in the battle of life, show them your bruises, particularly if part of your blown-away mouth looks ugly. It is always suffering but with a purpose. While the reed was on the floor, instead of resisting, it allowed shovels of dirt into it, and that dirt became strong stays that it would require in the future. Suffering is more than torn flesh or a bent leg, misshaped foot, or broken back. It has something to do with the deeper part of humans called "the human spirit."

Trials Put Something into Us

In the ground, the pipe occupied a tuning instrument. It discovered music it had never produced before in every dig of the spade or pull of the rake. The cutting edge of one tool was used to sharpen this reed into something more than what was blowing in the wind and hanging over the side of a river or stream. This ministry of music was no leaf blowing in the wind. The best music academy is where you find yourself blown by strong winds of opposition and sickness but not blown away but blown on—locked into a deeper experience with the Lord as you are blown back on course.

Never Surrender, Never Give In

When the apostle Paul had chains put on him (Colossians 4:3), he didn't surrender in his spirit. In prison he used his pen, parchment, prayer, and a personal witness. Grounded through any adventure, make sure that when you are found, you are still singing, for "sighing and mourning shall flee away" (Isaiah 51:11.) Fall like the apostle Paul when he was knocked off his donkey on the Damascus Road (Acts 9:3–4). It was in that falling and bruising that he heard the voice of Jesus. Sometimes the voice of Jesus speaking to us isn't found in trees and bees but in mud and sludge, rock and wrack. The voice of the Lord speaks to us in sinking, not swimming, as if every time we suffer, we hear a trumpet voice speaking to us. Then we go on as the bruised reed went on to live in the hands of its master musician.

In suffering people reach depths and heights than those who don't suffer never reach. That means in your suffering you have such a depth of understanding what Christ passed through on the cross when He died. The bruised reed had been where no other reed had been. It was in that position that it learned the music of the silent, falling tear. The salt in the falling tear is to remove any bitterness from our spirits. Always leave a space for forgiveness in your heart. "Father, forgive them; for they know not what they do" (Luke 23:34). There is such an experience as displaying the sufferings of Christ. We all want to share the life of Christ but not His sufferings. We want the medals without the colorful ribbons. I want to know Him and His sufferings (Philippians 3:10).

SUFFERING IS FOR OUR GOOD

Jacob was never the same after this experience. The man with one leg walked farther than he ever would with two legs. It was suffering that took the twist from his life and made it straight. It was suffering that produced the rose in him. It is the tightening of the strings that produces music. It was the blade of the knife that made such music in depth in the reed. That suffering was never a burden, because even at the end of Jacob's life, according to the book of Hebrews, he "worshipped leaning on top of his staff" (Hebrews 11:21). Notice that he was "on top" of his staff.

It says of Israel and their suffering, "They meant it for evil"—
that is, the Egyptians—but God "meant it" unto good (Genesis
50:20). It is a weaving term. That broken and torn thing is taken and
used as some material to produce a rare cloth. God is always taking
the broken strands of life and weaving them into the wholeness in
our lives.

If you think there is no limp in victory, speak to those who
climb high mountains and see the burns on their hands and feet,
and bruises on their bodies. Speak to those who walk the length of
Britain or parts of America to raise funds for good purposes; they
have swollen feet. They have aching limbs, but they made it; more
importantly, it made them. Some cycle through Great Britain and
France, who have sores received from the rubbing bicycle saddle.
You have all seen on labels on goods "Made in Britain" or "China"
or some other country. Over every life write, "Made in suffering." It
means you have proved that you can come through suffering, just
like the bruised reed, and have overcome all things and are enjoying
the "hidden Manna."

There Is Such Radiance in Being a Winner

The daughter had to work late. She knew it would be too late
to collect her son from school, so she decided to ask Grandma
whether she would collect the little grandson from the school gates.
The boy came out of the gates, singing and skipping, but Grandma
couldn't believe what she was seeing; she was quite shocked. Her
grandson, who had gone to school looking pristine and ordered, had
one stocking lower than the other. His hair was disheveled. His tie
was twisted around the back of his neck. His pants were lower than
they should have been. His face was muddy and bloody.

"What have they done to you during that rugby match?" she
asked. "Just look at you. You went to school looking like a prince,

and here you are looking like a toad." Grandma Barbara drew the boy into her bosom and sobbed.

The boy simply said, "It's all right, Grandma, we won! We won! We won by a mile!" His smile dropped off the end of his chin and then rose beyond the top of his head as if it hadn't found enough face space. To the boy, as to us, the suffering doesn't matter; it's what we achieve that matters. It is of little consequence in this life how much or little we suffer, if at the end of it we win; we are victorious. It is victory in suffering that puts a smile a mile wide on your face, which bad happenings can't wipe off. It goes deeper than your skin or face. Suffering puts a smile on your spirit that enlarges what might have been a prune into a large plum.

Fifteen

The Bruised Reed's Closeness to Its Savior

The security of the music pipe wasn't in itself; it was in the one who rescued it twice, held in the hand and then security sustained in the shepherd's garb. It was always the safest when it was in his hand. Music was sent from it as perfume from a flower. In the most difficult times, because it was in the hand of the sheep carer, it felt majestic in its music, and it brought balance, such as a pendulum brings to a clock, when the leader into green pastures felt that he required regulating in his emotions. As the sheep leader held it in his hand, so the pipe reed held the shepherd in its hand, and those of different natures became one.

THE REED AT THE SHEPHERD'S "BECK AND CALL"

It would never again grow by the riverside or reach upward by the side of the flock. It would never alone enter new pastures. Carried along wherever he went, being close to the leader of sheep, it had to be always on call. It knew what the words meant in the phrase "beck and call." The reed was the "beck," taken from the "brook," and the leader of lambs was the "call." There was no sacredness that it wasn't free; the security and sacredness of his presence meant it could leave things to be worked "out" for it, through him who had worked things "into" it. If he fell, the reed would fall.

Be assured, believer, that all items are kept secure because of His power (Colossians 1:16–17). This lamb lover illustrates Jesus and the believer. "He upholds all things by the word of His power." It means you don't need to worry; He has signed you off. The One who has brought you in will take you on, and the One who takes you on will ultimately take you through everything that comes against you. It was in dire circumstances that the flag felt the power of the leader's presence. That reed, like you, became the sheep gatherer's treasure in the palm of his hand.

It Is Closeness to Christ That Counts

It was this closeness to the pastor that opened new pathways for the flute. The reed was just one piece of the path, the same dull color. Being in the master's hand meant that a new world blossomed before it, a world on expectation built on the tunes that he played. The one who carried it was its map of peace. In that sheep carer were the paths of righteousness. The path of hope was there; the path and place of achievement would come later. The different types of music came from the same source that had marked the reed with a knife. Sometimes it is the lamb's friend's knife in one hand and the reed in the other. Tunes and torment brought together need to be met, and newness is from the same source, sometimes where it might not have wanted to go. On other occasions, taken to such beautiful places, as one day, is the Christian heaven, that beautiful city that has the beauty of every human, beast, flower, and bird placed into it (John 14:1).

Terry Atkinson

BEAUTIFULLY DESIGNED BY CHRIST

There is beauty and grace when held in the palm of Christ. The carpenter of Nazareth is well trained to train you. From Him come the purposes of God, as from the hand of this reed holder came direction and duty. The hand that formed the leaf and put more lines on one leaf than another is the same hand marking your life with grace. He gives liberally. There is no holding back when Jesus gives to us. He gives abundantly and freely.

There had to be that experience of nothing between for revealed glory. Not even the thickness of the wind had to be there. Its music must not mingle with the songs of the birds or the bleat of the sheep.

Being near its creator meant scales ascended as the music matured, so the Shepherd, as with you, can go higher or lower. This reed's life is a life set to pastoral music. Music without a musician is a sorry sight. If it isn't available, that musical instrument becomes a museum piece. We need the Master's touch so our range of living can expand from mud into music.

THE UGLIEST CAN BECOME CINDERELLA

From what had been such an ugly thing, something so common became beautiful. The fingers that held it and the lips that touched it with a kiss transformed stick to a song, since it became more than a conductor's baton The breath was forced through it, and this common river reed produced such beautiful melodies. These songs married to tunes weren't melodies of mud and mire but melodies of moments of the sheer joy of majesty.

It had no eyes but his eyes. It has no feet but his feet. It had no mouth but his mouth. It had no heart but his heart. It was dependent on the anointer of sheep. They became twins as a river is to water or a sunbeam to the sun. As a midge lives in a sunbeam, so this reed lived, moved, and had its being in the one who carried it (Acts

17:28). The one who carried it cared for it more than he cared for many sheep, because under his guidance it could do what no sheep could do. There was more than the spring of the lamb or the wiggle of its tail when sucking milk.

DEPEND ON CHRIST

In the lamb's leader, there was always the strength that a hollow pipe lacked. It was being carried by one whose power wouldn't fail to carry it through. Atlas, who could lift the world, had saved this forlorn, feeble flute from a watery grave. Because it was close to him, the cruel hand of Mother Nature would never let it be mere dust. It was now part of something more enduring than dust and water. It didn't feel like a hollow, cold, watery tube. It was part of the sheep rescuer and part of a moving, living, talking body. It found stability by being with the stable one, the one who seemed to know every nook and cranny and every pathway they came across. It always seemed as if he had been there before. It reminds us of one who said, "For me to live is Christ" (Philippians 1:21). He lived, breathed, talked, and walked Christ. Wherever the music reed was positioned, it was the kind man who was the nearest. It was as dependent on him as we are on Christ. This reed flute became the sheep gatherer's bandstand.

GOD ALWAYS KNOWS WHERE HE IS LEADING YOU

As it nurtured into maturity, it was evident that the person of river crossing and streams knew what he was doing and where he was going. The Carrier will always bring a sense of security to us when we lack clarity and direction and when we trust the hand that holds us. Let His hands do the holding and let His feet do the walking. Let His lips produce the melody in your moments of dire despondency.

It knew the words well: "from dust thou art and unto dust shalt thou return" (Genesis 3:19), but in between times it would be free to fill a new world with music, just a word uttered in musical form.

As the shepherd's emotions translated from being discouraged into a higher mood, a mood of victory in the shadow of defeat, he felt better. The sun shone again on every leaf and flower. Into something more sublime than what might slip off the edge of the table, the pastoral tube was transformed.

MY GOD SHALL SUPPLY ALL YOUR NEEDS

In that nearness to its dearest, he would supply the breath and the music for the stalk, just like a prisoner set free who has served a lifetime in solitude. As the reed went everywhere, it made music wherever it went. Whatever the circumstance, whatever the weather, no matter how depressed the lamb's master felt, the pipe would let its music sound out, and that was enough, since music scattered melancholy.

The heartbeat and pulse of the fleece grower converted into musical melodies. It learned its dancing moves. It was taught new themes daily and hourly, because of its nearness to the pastor. This stalk was the shepherd's body, soul, and spirit. In his love of it, that love became its heart, strength, soul, and mind (Luke 10:27).

Only this sustainer of sheep could decorate each day with new aspects of love. From that small tube came glorious themes. What nature provided, the tube blower took and converted into music. A tune quieted each blowing wind or raging storm. Radiant sunshine transposed into music. Music to the leader was like food, breakfast, dinner, tea, and supper—all in one.

Instead of taking a break or going on a holiday, he played a tune. His break time was a musical interlude. As the pasture man played, everything became part of a new creation with new dimensions.

Each experience the pastor entered, it was translated into music. Bad times, good times, great times, short times—they were all part of the next composition. Through the reed's music, gray skies became colorful rainbows. Its music was so rich and rare in his hands, and it could cause wounded birds to fly again. It brought the experience to the shepherd that we should bring to others, since it made water flow from a rock. Difficult experiences transformed. All were part of its ministry. The shepherd enjoyed it, but because of its closeness and usefulness the pipe flute was to its player, it became of it all.

That pipe was the man of the sheep's musical stage. Each day was a new performance. What blocked their way suddenly became waters they could sail through. It was as if, through this musical instrument, Moses had struck the rock, and water came out abundantly (Numbers 20:11). Where there was a drought in the sheep keeper's spirit, it poured water. Through its ability in his hands, it saw manna come from the earth (the unbeliever saw only dew) and quail come from the leaden skies (Exodus 16:13). If it had ears, it would hear every conversation the lamb lover ever had with the sheep (Mark 4:9). If you listen hard enough, even without ears, you will hear Him speak to you, words to the weary that refresh, speaking through the reed in his hands to the lame. "You can walk and run and not be weary." Don't "faint," by the way. Don't "cave" in when you get into a cave and can't get out or through. Men should always pray and not "faint"—in other words, "cave in" (Luke 18:1).

THE MUSIC OF GRACE CAN SHORTEN THE RACE

The legs of the leader would take it on long journeys, step by step, steep by steep, hour by hour. Sweat would be the only drinking water some days in the heat of the moment and mountain. If the journey was downhill, uphill, through the thorny bush or a field of flowers, everything was OK and not K.O.

The long distances were made shorter by tunes as the flag played. It made the long journey more straightforward. Like a smile, it converted the smile into a laugh. As the sheep director played, the desert blossomed like a rose. The barren began to sing the song of the redeemed. Where nothing grew, everything started to grow, as melody after melody sounded out into the highways and byways. That barren place became fruitful because of the nearest and dearest of the feeder and carer and reed. You can "do" and "be" in the hands of Jesus Christ. Jesus isn't looking for another pipe of music; He has found you. He wants the moods of harmony to flow through you as water pours along a riverbed and empties itself into the vast ocean. Let each finger on that hand be another musical note, and you will float where you would normally sink. Let His presence float your boat.

THE LORD ORDERS STEPS

"A man's heart deviseth his way: but the Lord directeth his steps" (Proverbs 16:9). "The steps of a good man are ordered by the Lord: and he delighteth in his way" (Psalm 37:23). As with us, it isn't the steps that cause us great difficulty as being tricky; sometimes when we are climbing Mount Everest, it is between the steps that we require the most help. It is then that we seem to slip back into our old ways of talking, doing, and being. If the leader should slip, the reed was in a secret, secure place. He had made sure that in any eventuality and calamity, it would be safe. The music couldn't be blown away forever. No wind could blow it out of its security, never lost in a forest of trees. The discerning leader knew the difference between sheep and the slim reed. The pipe didn't need to hang on. The music player pocketed it, placed where it was sometimes for a rainy day.

If the leader went to rescue a sheep, this disciple also went with him. If the stone and sling aimed at the enemy should miss its target, the reed was secure in him. If the rod and staff were called into action, the reed was there—not to help, for it couldn't work in certain circumstances, but it could watch and marvel at the ability of the sheep leader. He was called the "good shepherd"; he was good to men and sheep, flute, and lambs.

SAVED TO SERVE

The music stalk had someone who would do everything for it if it remained as it created music. Jesus Christ said, "I will never leave you nor forsake you" (Matthew 28:20). He is saying to you, "Lo, I am with you always." That means through every type of weather you know (whether or not)! In Psalm 23:4 we read, "For thou art with me." In the Hebrew language, there is no "art with." It is merely coming through death valley—"thou," "me." Climbing the highest mountain, there are Him and me. As a penny in a purse, so am I in God.

WRAPPED IN HIS LOVE AS A GARMENT

The reed was close, hidden within his garment or near to his heart, in a special place, decided by the fingers that had plucked it from the side of the river to be always at the sheep shearer's side. This truth reminds us that the garment of His righteousness covers us. It is a seamless dress. It was without a seam, woven from the top throughout (John 19:23), woven from top to bottom without any joint in it. It is made to fit all and to be used for all purposes. Don't put your best dress or suit on when going somewhere special, but put on His garment of righteousness; that is a garment of praise. His holiness will bring you warmth and security. When you act righteously, you are near to His heart. Live as one of His heartbeats.

The woman with the issue of blood could only "touch" the hem of Jesus's garment (Matthew 9:20). But this reed was "in touch" with the shepherd just as we are "in touch" with Jesus Christ. Within reach, we reach, allowing His fingers to touch us and help us to be something quite different from what we used to be. It was in the folds of his garment with him. We are required to be there because we always need another touch, so He can reach, He can teach, and He can teach from His reach.

Always Be in Touch with the Almighty God

Psalm 91:1 says that those who "dwelleth in the secret place of the most High shall abide under the shadow of the Almighty." This has the meaning of "being in touch with the almightiness of God." It is this connection that makes us strong and brave. He touches us to touch others. You can reach only when reached; you can touch only when you are touched. You can teach only when taught. We can all sound out the music of His majesty as we praise Him in our walk, talk, and through our tune. Our melodies of the heart, making melody in our hearts to the Lord, come from the same hymn sheet—Him and His book (Ephesians 5:19).

We have a promise that Jesus will never leave us or forsake us (Hebrews 13:5). I will never keep on leaving you and forsaking you—no, not for a split second. He will never leave us in the lurch. "That where I am, there shall you be also"; they might be there also (John 14:3). What I am and where I am isn't dependent on me. They are dependent on Jesus Christ. For every move the musician made, the reed was involved in that move.

He pulled it from its secure position, and it became an apostle of music, for music would be sent from it. It was there as the sheep keeper's representative. This tube was his forerunner and brother. What was in the shepherd's heart was played on the shepherd's pipe.

Sixteen

The Bruised Reed's
Body Ministries

There were certain things only the reed could do that would help
the disgruntled man. Being with the pasture provider through
vale, vulnerability, and over hills and far away, it was always there to
be a help to the shepherd of the sheep. What the pipe stick did for
the man of the wool, you can do for the true Shepherd of the sheep,
Jesus Christ. In how and when it helped him, you can help the body
of Christ (Ephesians 4:11). You can minister in your church, helping
others who are in the lurch, unable to make progress, even that of
the worm or snail. The grass stalk would always be a stick of music
to listen to during a time of weakness.

Never talk yourself down. It was only a reed. It was the finest of
its type because it was selected and secured. From it came streams in
the desert, the best of its kind, because of the kindness of its handler.
It contained such a ministry that weeping willows, when they heard
it, ceased weeping. Those who had put their harps on the branches of
the willow tree took them down and began to play songs of security
(Psalm 137:2).

Through the reed's ministry into misery, it produced hope in
the hopeless, putting new strength into the weak. It became manna

to those in the wilderness. These are parts of your ministry and will bring you to your destiny.

Yours Is a Ministry Gift

The pipe had no ministry, only that proved by the lamb lover. As God gives fruit to trees and flower heads to stems, He has granted you a ministry that is solely yours. Don't compare what you have with another. Use and be used. You can be the painter of rainbows across somebody's dark sky. Its music was about him or her; the same applies to us in our relationship with Christ, the Shepherd. We have no breath but His breath. We have no music but His music. We become His song, lovely in the altogether lovely. We, through His grace, become His eyes, mouth, ears, feet, and hands.

Let those hands be cups full of water. Let those eyes be eyes of vision, leading the blind into sight, feet walking steadily along, taking others with them. Let your mouth be the spokesperson of God. Sing, for the glory of heaven has filled your soul.

Behold, All Things Become New

Every time the reed was lifted from the sheep gatherer's clothing, there was something new that came from it. The traveler's pipe was no fish in stagnant waters. What was heard wasn't an old ditty or a worn-out chorus. The writer of Psalms said, "I will sing unto the Lord a new song" (Psalm 33:3; 96:1). There is nothing stale about a new composition, a composition into a dreary position that sets people free. When the road became rough and steep, unsteady, and unready for those not so ready, it brought the reed into its ministry. Through its music, it could make footprints for the shepherd to follow. Each musical sound could be part of a march—not into the valley of death but up the mountain of hope. Walking to the beat of the music lifted him as if angels' wings were under him.

Yours Is a Ministry between Two

Sometimes ministry is only between two people. That is private, and it is perceptive; it is persuasive. It can take those in the valley of despair to the pinnacle of hope. Not many people commit suicide by leaping from the mountain of hope. The person is in need, and the pipe reed can meet that need. When any condition required reed ministry, it was "pressed down, and shaken together, and running over" (Luke 6:38). Ministry is sometimes committed only to, and seen in, those who only stand and wait, since the reed was always there, ready with a lilt, lullaby, or new tune. What sounded out from it to encourage all who heard it was a lullaby of love. Strength and praise poured through it. It was the reed's way of saying thank you. We must be available in our availability—found in our ability, as released into us, and working through us from our guide of the sheep.

Your Ministry Is to Christ First and Last

Always remember that the ministry of the flute was first to the shepherd and then to the sheep. It is essential to get the order correct. You need to do for Jesus Christ and His body of believers whatever they require. Whenever there was a need, the pipe was waiting ready like the starter's pistol to commence a race, prepared as the athlete to run that race or a bird to fly into the unknown.

The miracle ministry of the flute was its ability to put new life into old situations. It set new vigor into the shepherd, who was about to faint because of the rigor. It became the one who fulfilled the exhortation "wherefore lift up hands which hang down and the weak knees" (Hebrews 12:12). It could speak a word in music form, using the language of the heart, sending out a tune to him who was weary. Through the music played, words of knowledge and wisdom went forth. To those who don't understand the vigor or color of music, it spoke in another language. This flag was able to interpret everything placed in it as the breath of the shepherd came through it. It put new paint onto fading pictures. It brought laughter and cheer, not painted onto the face. What splashed on couldn't be washed off. It produced new vigor of virtue.

Certain qualities are in the body of Christ, those qualities sometimes found in a bruised reed. They were located in Quartus, a brother (Romans 16:23), whose name means "a quarter." There is room here for the small and the tall. Quartus, a man, was determined, like Zacchaeus, to grow through a tree (Luke 19:1–10). You, as a bruised reed, are one of these ministries. It is ministry into the heart, sometimes the mind—on other occasions to the spirit, soul, and body. Because you have been bruised, to the broken you are part of the ministry in your church. You may never be recognized or have a great title, referred to as "that old reed." That "old reed" was of the stoic breed.

Your Bruising Qualifies You for Ministry

It is your smallness and the fact that you are hurt many times that qualify you for your ministry into another's misery. You can get and go where others only dream of, as the music did from this green pipe.

People with broken hearts love to be ministered unto from a person with a broken heart. This ministry is like a burst of sunshine in the middle of a storm, ministry and giftings that keep the fire of devotion in others burning. Those who are cold can come and be warmed after freezing in a winter of discontent. Those who are as smoking flax require your music so they are unquenchable. Your ministry can stir up the embers in members.

Nobody has the talent you have for coming alongside others. As sweet, deep music sounding out into their misery, melancholy, maladies, and seeing God, the God of all mercies works through you, "for thou art a gracious and merciful God" (Nehemiah 9:31). Jesus Christ has taken "captivity captive" (Ephesians 4:8). That means He has taken those captive "by the sword," through His Word. Your greatest power. Your unknown ability. The secret weapon is the Word of God. The fact is that you have listened to His voice. It has been translated into music, responding with the music of His majesty.

You Are a Ministry Gift to the Body of Christ

The reed pipe was there as a gift. It had been redeemed, sought twice; and part of its redemption was thankful service. Jesus Christ has set ministries within the body of believers (Ephesians 4:11–12). There are apostles, prophets, teachers, pastors, and evangelists. There is the little ministry gift of "helps," which nobody seems to notice (1 Corinthians 12:28). The word *helps* means "support." The word suggests someone who runs alongside another, feeding and watering them with encouragement. When I am weak, will you be vulnerable with me? When I need help, will you be that help? The word *helps* describes those on the side of the running track who give food and water to the athlete. People used to be stationed near ice-covered ponds in England's deep winters, and they were there to help those out of the icy waters if they fell in. They were called "Helps."

This small stick of music could be so helpful if it were part of the ladder, the first rung when seeking to climb to success. Not only did the trees of the fields clap their hands, but when the reed played, great boulders that blocked the way also seemed to disintegrate, since they appeared to be crushed by music. You are the prop that looks like a pipe to others.

Terry Atkinson

THE BELIEVER CAN HELP TO MATURE OTHERS

As a reed pipe, be more than a pipe dream; you are a ministry gift. The reed would fulfill all the ministries Christ gave to His church, not as toys for boys but as weapons for warriors. Ministries have been provided for the "perfecting of the saints," meaning to "restore" a dislocated joint (Ephesians 4:12), meaning "perfect adjustment." Playing on the tube was ministry through music. When the sheep lover and leader felt he was falling apart, he was back together again, using a theme as cement and mortar.

The pipe fulfilled the role of the apostle through what the shepherd would do with it. It was the pipe with music that pioneered its way through the darkness, "doubt" ("to be pulled two ways"), fear, and terror (Matthew 14:31). It was a true pioneer, boldly going where music had never gone before, defeating empty echoes with sound songs. The possibility was that as it played, it could turn water into wine and fading grass into a new luster of green. When the sheep were trembling and the voice of the commander in chief couldn't calm them, out came the music pipe, and it was like a hand that grasped a raging sea and made it as serene as plastic. No one listened to birds chirping or singing when the tune was made known. How different the sounds it made to the piercing cry of eagle or hawk.

WITNESS A RESURRECTION IN YOUR LIFE

If it is true that the apostle must have witnessed the resurrection from the dead of Jesus Christ, this reed had done just that, lifted from the dead itself. In its natural state, it was heading for the autumn of death after growing at the side of the stream. It then knew of a shepherd who had come to it when it lost as one from the dead. Through and because of its ability to sound out music, it had seen men dead and buried raised again to new life. It had often seen the weary, worn leader sitting exhausted by the roadside, raised to walk, talk, laugh, and also work. This reed had itself been raised to new life and sought to repay the miracle by raising others into a new life.

Through Ministry, You Can Change the Future

Its music never stopped when they came to a river or stream. Whatever it passed through, whenever it was required, it exercised its nobility in music. The reed could prophesy the future, dismantling the posts that hemmed the shepherd in, posts and restrictions that restricted its owner's spirit. It could, just as the prophet, turn the tide of uncertainty and fear into tremendous hope against all the odds. It could take the guide and sheep from Death Valley to delightful Beulah Land. It was an actual seer through its music. It saw into problems and difficulties, but it also created a way through. It wasn't its ministry into the majesty that saw people as they were and criticized them. Rolling up its sleeves, it began to let music flow through it. The reed, when it saw a need, pulled out of the shadow of another to send forth its resplendent tunes.

The reed's secret for such music was that it was empty of itself when the sheep wept, every time calling out. The reassurer's hand trembled as the tuner and player held the flag in his hand; it was its music that prophesied of a better future.

It was able to light up a dark sky on a night. The reed would light a torch that would never go out. If the shepherd had breath, the reed had good music. It was an expression of its master. It was always opening red seas, as the flock faced failure. It said to the sheep, "We can do it."

You Can Lead and Feed Other Believers

The reed was a great pastor and orator. It spoke to the heart while other sounds just appealed to the mind, while some echoing sounds in the valley shot over the head of the sheep. The music coming from it plugged into the heart. Through its music, it could feed the narrow spirit of both sheep and shepherd. It could lead from the front. The musical interlude was the manna from heaven in music. Through one small reed, a choir filled the countryside in musical splendor. In deep winter, it could turn it into a spring married to summer.

It was a pastor to the pastor-shepherd, helping him in a time of conflict within his soul. It cared for others, each as if they were the only one. It was the reed that fed the spirit of the musician. He was as blessed as the sheep, more blessed than when twin lambs appeared. I was this, a small thing, that said, "All, all is well." Only a reed like this could spread a table in the wilderness and fill it with the food of love (Psalm 23:5).

Ministry through You Teaches Others

Did anything among the shepherds teach tranquility like this reed? It was a teacher in its music. The notes, marched from its emptiness as breath, were breathed into it as soldiers with their section of brass that played music to conquering armies. As the keeper and leader of lambs' hearts opened through its music, it put lessons learned into those hearts. The soul became the classroom for learning. It was saying to each, "Trust and don't be afraid." If its music should fail, as with your ministry, all would fail. This was the cornerstone to build on. It taught shepherd and sheep that everything would be all right, the outcome assured. It taught that the thing that did happen last time wouldn't engulf them as a wolf that bites them—teaching through its music, serenity, and surrender to the shepherd. What a ministry is ours in our availability to our Shepherd! Yours is the privilege of being a teacher in the body of Christ.

You Can Unite Those Apart from God

What a great evangelist it was. This reed pipe could untie; it could bring things together again that had been long separated. It could ensure the safety of any lamb caught in the mud that rescue was at hand. The gospel of the pipe reed was its music, reaching the unreachable and teaching the unteachable. Every opportunity was golden and musical. It searched out the unsearchable and brought them closer to the leader. When things would split apart and everything would run amok everywhere, under the powerful persuasion of the pipe, all were brought into a pasture of green grass and to quiet waters.

The reed was of quiet help to the helpless. From that one word *help*, a thousand ministries are expanded. It helped to turn dusk into daylight, darkness into light; and when any sheep was wounded, it became a soothing ointment. The key to the pipe's music was "If I can help somebody." It didn't matter what time of the day or night it was; it was always there ready, willing, and able to help, always on standby to help those who felt they couldn't stand. Through its music, it became the assistant to everybody. It could, through help given, calm everybody down, from shepherd to sheep.

Always Be Close to His Heart

When the reed was laid on one side or placed near the heart of the man of wool, so close that it could hear it as a drumbeat and call to war, it passed by his face and mouth after being lifted there. It could glance at the sleeping pioneer's eyes and see that all was well when that had been unwell. It was sometimes placed inside his tunic, knowing full well that it had played its part in bringing peace from perplexity. It is good each night, when work ceases, to feel the hand of Jesus, to know that His hand has been your platform for good. Knowing that you have been helping, caring, and building

Terry Atkinson

throughout your day, you can rest just as a reed pipe in a pocket or gown. It had no requirement to declare, "It is finished" (John 19:30); it knew that through its music, it had reached parts no other could reach. It had fulfilled its ministry—not to the letter of the law but to the strengthening of love.

Learn to Pray Morning and Evening

The reed passed by the face of the shepherd. The one who had created it, this pastoral thing, looked upon his face. It glanced at the lovely face of its creator and instigator. Always learn in your ministry to look upon the face of Christ before you retire. Experience what the flag of tunes experienced each evening as it looked upon his face. Before you place yourself in a position of rest and your music ceases for the day, look upon His face.

As the soldiers went out of the city, each of them looked upon the face of King David (2 Samuel 18:1–4). Little wonder that they could say, "Now thou art worth ten thousand of us." The winning of the war was in the face they looked upon as they passed by into battle. Take into every battle your last look on the face of Jesus Christ, and all will be well. All will be doubly well. The rescuer will always be the key player in the calling we are following. The same hand that fed the sheep also took care of the reed. That reed had a ministry, such as you, if only you will ask God to lead you into it. It wasn't the size of the tube of tunes that gave it its ability but the hand of the shepherd, since it is the hand of God that enables you to be what He has called you to be. You have now come into a more in-depth understanding of why you must be bruised. Born out of that suffering are the ministries of the reed flowing as music.

Seventeen

The Bruised Reed Coming into Deep Waters

There were many times when the reed of music had to pass through deep waters. Those waters were between the River Jordan and the Red Sea, from rivulets to rivers, then from ponds to lakes, and even to noisy streams that were anything but musical. The greatest fear of the sheep was when the rains sent rivers cascading down the mountainside; and as the stream flowed, it struck the rocks, making loud noises. The sheep were always afraid of noisy waters with waves like blades or shark's teeth.

LEAVE YOUR FUTURE TO THE GOD OF THE FUTURE

The pipe reed had no idea where it would be in the next step of the journey. We aren't aware what the Lord has planned for us, and sometimes He doesn't reveal that plan all at once; He reveals it little by little, bit by bit. If it were, as with these animals, revealed to us in a second, we would buckle at the knees. God is kind when He shields us with bends and corners so we can't see what is ahead of us. Never try to catch up with your future or past. Please leave it to the Almighty. The flock, led step by step, learn to walk with God and move at His pace into His place.

Terry Atkinson

When You Are Uncertain, Trust God

There were some streams and rivers where stepping-stones wouldn't have been adequate; they would have become stumbling blocks and not rowing boats, because the waters were too deep.

If you are going to measure the depth of dark waters you are going through, let the dove of God move over the face of the deep waters (Genesis 1:2). Measure what you are experiencing—not by the experience itself but through His love, because He loves you through and through-through everything. The reed was carried through by its friend to the other side. You are not only carried through, but you are tied to Him by a cord of love. The flock walked in the path of the ongoing man, who was going before them. You walk on in the light of the Lord; "walk as children of light" (Ephesians 5:8).

What Is Heavy to You Is Light to God

No matter what the herdsman had carried in the past, there would always be a place for the reed in the sheep carer's keeping. The reed of music was light when compared to heavy stuff the river crosser had carried. He had been training for this moment. His keeping power means that He "keeps His power." It means that His power is toward you to help during a time of stress (Ephesians 1:19; 3:20).

The leader was always more robust than the volume of swollen rivers. If you can't cross the stream where it is low, let Christ build you a bridge from His cross and cross there.

When Facing Deep Trouble, Look at the Lamb of God

To get across deep waters, the pastor sometimes took a lamb and placed it on his shoulders, just as he did with a sheep when rescuing it. It was always a token of victory when anything was carried high. When others in the flock saw the lamb, fear was bated, and calm repose came to them as a friend. The sheep needed his assurance because they knew of the dangers that could be in deep waters. As they saw shepherd and lamb, they followed.

Their victory is our victory. It was the closeness to the leader that brought them through deep waters. They didn't need to swim, row, or float but trust. When a wall was against them, they just kept going.

We need to keep our eyes fixed on Jesus, particularly when troubles become heaving waves of discontent that would turn us into a shipwreck Paul warned us against. "Concerning faith have made shipwreck" (1 Timothy 1:19). We all need a second look at Christ. Sometimes it takes three, four, five and many more times to realign our spiritual walk (Hebrews 12:2). "Looking" means "look away"; look away from the deep waters, from your troubles, from things of depth you don't understand. Instead of your gaze being full of what's gaunt and gruesome, look at His calm repose.

If He should slip and fall, the universe would collapse (Colossians 1:16). The stars would disintegrate and appear like a million spears of flame. Now, can't you trust Him to uphold all things by the word of his power (Colossians 1:16)?.

THE DEEPER THE TROUBLE, THE HIGHER HE LIFTS YOU

The fearful was lifted as a flag on a flagpole, carried as a flag of triumph by the conquering army. The deeper the waters, the higher the pipe music was lifted. When we pass through turbulent times, allow our Shepherd to lift us in grace; then the less likely we are to drown in our sorrows. Didn't Jehovah need to remind Israel that He bore them on eagles' wings (Exodus 19:4)? Always be reminded that He carries the map of the world, the map of your heart, of your world in His heart; and from it, He will never part. It is for double measure written on the palms of His hands. Do you know why it says when Jehovah was saying to Israel, "Lay these words 'in,' not 'on' your heart" (Deuteronomy 11:18)? If you "lay" His Word "on" your heart, He will break that heart, so that when broken, the Word of the Lord can fall into it and be sown as seed.

If He should sink in the mud, light would become darkness, and every rose would be a weed. Midnight would remain and rule forever. The only tune that would be ever played through the tube would be a funeral dirge.

God Wants You to Move into New Territory

Sometimes streams were natural borders that separated the land. When they passed through these waters, they were entering into new pastures and into an area where they might not have been before. Long-standing troubles can be the doorway into new and deeper experiences with the Lord. The sheep carer had left the grasses and gave them time to grow. In their absence, the sheep had grown. They were now able to feed on what the pastor had led them into. Don't resist trials and temptations; feed on them as green grass.

Better Things Are on the Other Side of Your Troubles

The best and greenest grasses were on the other side of the deep waters. Jesus said to those in the boat with Him, "Let us pass over unto the other side" (Mark 4:35). Learn to grow through your troubles, and if you do, your best moments of sheer pleasure will be before you. When gardening, mud and manure can produce such beautiful results, but even these watered can grow. There are things you have not tasted, yet that is in the hidden manna. There are gold nuggets to be collected in these dark waters. Remember, when Noah's ark went through the stormy waters, it was by the waves and storm that "it was lifted above the earth" (Genesis 7:17). The conclusion of its journey was on Mount Ararat.

There Is New Music on the Other Side

Jesus said to His disciples, "I will go before you and into Galilee" (Mark 14:28). It is sometimes called the Lake of Tiberius (John 21:1), "Tiberias" meaning "a harp." So Jesus was going to meet with them. It was a place that represented music in the shape of a harp. If only every deep sea and troubled waters became a harp. The reed felt as safe as the shepherd, because he was carrying it.

The pipe music needed not to sink below the turbulent waters; it had never been created to be a sailing boat or a sinking boat. Lord, teach me to float on top of my troubles and don't let them take me under but over. It is just as important that you keep your head above by being, as the tuned tube near your head, Christ Jesus. The waters will win the day if you give in and say, "I sink in life's alarms." Even the early believers had to pass through troubled waters. Shall not He who broke up the waters of the deep and created seas and oceans lose control over you as you are born along by His strength (Genesis 7:11)? He has promised. "When you come to, the waters, fear not; I am with you." "And he led them safely, so that they feared not" (Psalm 78:53). Sometimes it is water to the ankles. Then to the knees, up to the thighs, and then into deep depths—waters to swim in, not sink in (Ezekiel 47:3–6)!

God Prepares What You Are Passing Through

There are so many things in the book of Jonah that God "prepared"—a wind, a worm, a great wind, a whale. And He has prepared these waters for you (Jonah 1:17; 4:6–8). The one thing God couldn't prepare at the beginning was Jonah, the prophet, but God prevailed in the end. Only face paint and shallowness were washed away. The nearest thing by which the reed of music came to water was saliva from the shepherd's mouth and perspiration from his brow.

We must recognize the lordship of Christ, whether the waters are deep or shallow. There can be more danger in shallow waters for the reed and us than there is in deep, immeasurable racing torrents. When and where it is shallow, we think we can manage it all by ourselves. The moment we feel that, we begin to sink. The pipe had to be kept in a different disposition than that of water.

The Great Shepherd Will Carry You Through

Your troubles may have been long and deep; however deep or long, He knows how your troubles have been. Let the Lord of love carry you through. This brings a new feature to the words, as the reed was lifted higher, "He will see you through." He is the One who can take you step by step through it all. Don't try to run through water; if you do, you will be easily swept off your feet and be swept downriver to a cataract. When the water is more than christening sprinkling, you need the Almighty.

Treasured and Important Things Are Carried Aloft

You have witnessed soldiers carrying their weapons above their head as they have passed through deep waters. You will see some people carry their shoes, tied around their necks. What is important to people they will lift higher. As we travel through testing times of trouble, it is the capable Lord of the stream who will carry us through.

Ask the Lord of creation to carry you through. The One who created the roaring river also made the silent tear. Both need to be requested and required. If He does, it will mean that you don't need to walk across water or on water. The reed wasn't lifted higher by its hand but by its master's hand. The pipe didn't need to cling on for dear life. It was the grip of the music player that held it high. The one who got the notes of music correct would also get things right when passing through a deep river.

We are called, even when trouble is as the seven seas and as large as an ocean of opposition, to let Him do the holding. There is peace like a river when we realize God, the Shepherd, is holding on to us. Christ upholds all things by the word of His power (Colossians 1:16).

The reed had no legs or eyes, as we stated in an earlier chapter. It was the legs, eyes, hands, and arms of the powerful shepherd that carried it along. Better than a boat floating on the waves, it wasn't the worrying of the flag that brought it to the other side of the lake. It isn't our capabilities or crisis moments that will bring us to the other side of this life.

THE MUSIC REED CARED FOR AS A PET LAMB

What the leader didn't do was throw the reed over to the other side, then come and collect it. That throw would have bruised it, and it could have landed anywhere. The one who could forge water took it as a pet lamb. As those sheep grew wool for the shepherd, so the water reed produced music. His clothes were as wet as the waves, and the torrent hit him but not the secret pipe of music. It was safer than safe, more secure than security.

Your pastor isn't the only way, but He is the bridge over troubled waters. You, being born along by Christ, can look down on troubled waters. To lose it, as we have discovered, would have been like losing a best friend. It had learned to lean on the strength of the shepherd's breast. Wasn't it the apostle John who relied on the bosom of Jesus at the Last Supper (John 13:23)? One word in the Old Testament translated "lean" means "strength" or "rest" (Song of Solomon 8:5).

You don't get across stormy waters by shouting or wishing but by somebody else doing something for you that lifts you higher. The pipe of music was lifted higher and higher. The greater the swell of water, the higher it came, and higher the pipe was lifted. If your troubles are too many to count, you can count on Christ. He can lift you higher so that nothing touches you, but it wets Him through. He can lift you through because He died on a cross.

WHATEVER TROUBLES YOU TROUBLES CHRIST FIRST

Anything that might have touched and rushed the music stem touched the leader first. He could face what this pipe could never face. He has been "touched" with the feelings of your infirmities (Hebrews 4:15; 5:2). He was covered in darkness for three hours so you might play "light" music.

The waters that surround us can test our faith. We must come through every deep and injurious temptation as that inside Noah's ark, for this reed was as secure. These waters, if you let Jesus lift you so high that you crown Him with a crown of it will never wash away what is between you and your Lord. Have such a deep experience that it can't wash away in a torrent of water.

The shepherd would never allow the pipe from himself. The deeper the waters, the higher the reed must go. It is from the position of the highlands of Canaan that we can see walls of water, like those walls around Jericho thrown down (Joshua 6:5).

LET JESUS TAKE THE TROUBLE OUT OF TROUBLE

It is good to accept that what happened to this music stick can happen to you. When danger threatens, there is no fear in the valiant man's heart. He has passed this way many times before. He knows where the rapid is less powerful. He knows where and when the waters aren't in full flood (Joshua 3:15–16). The Shepherd, who is ours, knows where it's shallow or deep. He sometimes avoids the "time of the flood."

Christ knows when you aren't ready for deep waters, the deep waters of faith. We can barely accept the gentle waters of the potter as the vessel of clay is being formed. He will take you through the icy waters and hallow them. You may come into the waters that surround you as a minnow, trying to swim your way through, but go through as a whale of Jonah fashion. Go through as that ship called *Dreadnought*! Go through, being carried as a salmon going upstream, not by self-effort but by being carried along. It is so sad that the only time some of us allow ourselves to be carried along is inside a coffin. But best of all, come through storms, like Jonah who was fast asleep was fast "asleep" in the side of the ship (Jonah 1:5). The word used here means "deep sleep."

THROUGH SUFFERING, YOU CAN SEE HIS FACE MORE CLEARLY

All the water will do for the Shepherd is wash His face so the reed can see Him more clearly. Feel Him wrap His being around you as you pass through many waters. You will pass through this day as dry as a stick because you are called to bear a cross made of wood.

The writer to the Hebrews speaks of a "forerunner" who has gone before us (Hebrews 6:20). In New Testament times, fogs and deep mist used to cover some ports so large ships couldn't enter. The "forerunner" was a small vessel, dispatched to take hold of the cable attached to the larger vessel. The "forerunner," Jesus Christ, draws us through mist and fog, from water and worry, into the port of our destination. All they had to do in the large ship, as you in your torment, was to keep their eyes on the "forerunner."

Terry Atkinson

THE SAFEST PLACE IN THE WORLD

The safest place in the world isn't in the world; it's in the Word, Jesus Christ (John 1:1). It's not in the water, whether cold or hot, stagnant or fresh. It's in knowing the closeness of Christ; as you enter trouble, He begins to lift you above that trouble. That is why in Colossians 3:1 we must seek those things that are above. Eve's place was alongside Adam as a helpmeet (Genesis 2:18), removed from the side of Adam to be his equal. This isn't so for us as Christians. We are lifted higher than we deserve. It is only faith that will take us to the highest heaven when passing through the deepest hell.

FACE OPPOSITION IN THE ECHO OF HIS VOICE

God, through your troubles, is the echo of the voice of your Shepherd, who is calling you over, taking you over, or talking you over to where the grass is greener on the other side. He is carrying you over, not letting you go under. Water can't separate you from the love of God (Romans 8:35–39). It means that if you acknowledge Him and He lifts you higher, you won't sink, to be remembered no more. You will pass over the brook Kidron as the disciples did as they went into the garden of Gethsemane (John 18:1); and you will find that there are angels there, waiting to strengthen you. Every wave of torment can become the wing of an angel if it has wings.

The Chief Shepherd who took you in will bring you through, and as those three Hebrew lads had no smell of fire on them after going into a fiery furnace (Daniel 3:27), there won't even be a damp patch on you after you have come through the waters of affliction. Streams, streamlets, and surges of water or sewers will never sweep sovereignty away.

Printed in the United States
By Bookmasters